RESTORATION REWARDED

A Celebration of Railway Architecture

40 YEARS OF THE NATIONAL RAILWAY HERITAGE AWARDS

ROBIN LELEUX

UNIQUE BOOKS

First published in the United Kingdom
by Unique Books 2019

© Text: Robin Leleux 2019

© Photographs: As credited

ISBN: 978 0 9957493 7 5

All rights reserved. No part of this book may be reproduced or transmitted in any form or by any means electronic or mechanical, including photocopying, recording or by any information storage without permission from the Publisher in writing. All enquiries should be directed to the Publisher.

A CIP record for this book is available from the British Library

Unique Books is an imprint of Unique Publishing Services Ltd,

3 Merton Court, The Strand, Brighton Marina Village, Brighton BN2 5XY.

www.uniquebooks.pub

Designed by Ian Hughes, www.mousematdesign.com

Printed in Poland

Acknowledgements

The Awards Management Committee passed the production of this book to a small group comprising Theo Steel, Peter Waller and me. I was entrusted with writing the main text and many of the captions; however I am most grateful to Peter and Theo for their ready guidance and assistance, with sourcing pictures and to Peter for seeing the book through to publication. Most pictures are from the Awards archive, which comprises photographs taken by our judges over the years, and the photographer is credited where known as are other suppliers of pictures. However, there are inevitably some gaps, so if we have inadvertently missed anyone off, please accept both our thanks and our apologies. Finally, over many years, Claire Picton, from the RHT, has been an immense help to the NRHA; it is appropriate that we express our gratitude to her at this time.

Robin Leleux
July 2019

Contents

Foreword by Gordon Biddle	3
Preface by John Ellis	4
1: In the Beginning 1979–1983	5
Conversion to Accommodation	12
2: A Widening Remit 1983–1989	14
Conversion to Pubs and Cafés	22
3: Using the Past to Serve the Future 1989–1994	26
Bridges and Tunnels	36
4: Towards Independence 1995–1999	42
Memorials and Miscellaneous	56
5: Charitable Status 2000–2004	64
New Build	82
6: Playing an Important Role 2004–2019	86
Plaque Unveilings	122
Appendix 1: Presentation Ceremony Venues and Guests of Honour	123
Appendix 2: Sponsors	125
Appendix 3: Judges and Adjudicators	126
Index of Locations	127

Front cover – above: Arley station, on the preserved Severn Valley Railway, has featured regularly as an award winner over the 40 years of the competition. *NRHA*

Front cover – below: The work undertaken on the Midland Hotel and St Pancras station during the 1990s resulted in one of the most spectacular restorations in the past 30 years. *Allan Damiral*

Back cover: Over the years a significant number of signal boxes have featured in the competition; that at Kirkham Abbey on the York to Scarborough line was a winner in 2011. *Robin Leleux*

Foreword

By Gordon Biddle

I well remember a day in 1979 when the late Michael Harris phoned me at my office in London to say he would like to talk about a project he had in mind. He was editor of *Railway World* and I had come to know him through having contributed several articles about Victorian railway architects and architecture. I invited him around for coffee a few days later, when we discussed the idea of awards for restoration work at stations of preserved railways. The result was the Best Preserved Station Competition, soon to be renamed the Best Restored Station Competition and now, as the following pages will show, widened in scope to become the Railway Heritage Awards. Neither of us imagined that forty years later they would still be going strong. Numerous other people prominent in the world of railways have given active support and encouragement in that time. Whilst it may be a trifle invidious to single out individuals, I feel I must mention three without whose help the project could well have foundered: Captain Peter Manisty, RN; Bernard Kaukas, at that time chief architect of British Rail; and David Allan, managing director of the publishers Ian Allan Ltd.

Gordon Biddle

With his professional background in land surveying and building construction, working in both local government and the insurance business, Gordon Biddle was well placed to write a definitive history of the *Railway Surveyors* (1990), just one of his fourteen books on inland waterways and railway civil engineering and architecture. Having co-edited the *Oxford Companion to British Railway History* with the late Prof. Jack Simmons, he produced probably his *magnum opus*, *Britain's Historic Railway Buildings* in 2003. His latest book is *Two hundred years of the Lancaster Canal: an illustrated history* published in 2018. As well as founding the National Railway Heritage Awards and playing an active role in its affairs for many years, he helped to found the Railway & Canal Historical Society in 1954, and is currently a vice-president. He is also a Fellow of the Royal Society of Arts.

Right: Gordon Biddle

Preface

By John Ellis

I joined BR in 1962 as a graduate management trainee, having obtained a degree in Philosophy, Politics and Economics at Oxford. I had no previous predilection towards railways, but a strong interest in transport economics. I thought that the post Beeching era would represent career opportunities, and I liked the modernisation element of the report.

My first post after training was as Assistant Station Master at Cardiff General (then, now Central) station, a fine listed structure, largely unchanged today. Then followed several posts in freight operating and marketing, before a move to Board HQ at 222 Marylebone Road (now the Landmark Hotel) as Passenger Promotions Officer followed by a move to the Southern at Waterloo. Thence to Commercial Manager in the King's Cross Division of the Eastern Region, where we saw the introduction of HSTs. A move back to freight followed at Eastern Region's HQ at York (yet another listed building, also now a Hotel).

My first general management post was Divisional Manager, Liverpool Street based in the now demolished Hamilton House in Bishopsgate, when the redevelopment of the station was beginning. This was followed by a move back to Southern as Deputy General Manager to Gordon Pettitt, where I oversaw the redevelopments of Charing Cross, Cannon Street and Victoria. Then followed a move to General Manager, Scotland, back to Waterloo as General Manager, thence to Inter City as Deputy MD, to Railtrack as Production Director, finally back to Scotland as MD of the Scotrail train operator.

After retirement I was persuaded by Jim Cornell to become Chairman of the NRHA Committee and have enjoyed 20 years of guiding the work of the Committee, the fruits of whose work you see in this book. It has been great fun, and a wonderful experience. My best wishes to all who continue to carry on the work of the Committee.

John Ellis,
Chairman,
National Railway Heritage Awards
July 2019

John Ellis. *Duncan Phillips/NRHA*

CHAPTER 1

In the Beginning 1979–1983

Flying Scotsman and *King George V* were busy steaming the BR rails in the early 1970s, to be joined by other restored former BR steam locomotives as the demand for steam-hauled railtours grew. Meanwhile the 'preserved railways', following the lead set in previous decades first by the Talyllyn and Ffestiniog railways then by the Bluebell and Keighley & Worth Valley lines, were developing rapidly from Kent and Somerset to Yorkshire, across into Shropshire and into Wales, and up into Scotland too. They offered their customers a steam-hauled ride, increasingly with restored former BR locomotives, along parts of branch lines which had mostly been pruned from the national network by the Beeching reshaping in the 1960s. However, one significant feature was lacking: stations. With all the emphasis on restoring steam locomotives to working order, often little was being done about the structures on the branch lines which were in danger

Above: This inscribed slate plaque, designed by Alan Breeze, was the first to be won in the Awards, for Oakworth Station. *Robin Leleux*

Michael Harris (1945–2001)

Author, journalist and transport campaigner, Michael Harris had an early career with BR and English Electric Traction before joining the Ian Allan publishing house, first as editor of its popular magazine *Railway World* (he did two stints at this), then as editorial director and finally as Managing Director before becoming a transport consultant. Meanwhile he also assisted (1973) with the founding of Transport 2000 (now known as the Campaign for Better Transport) to press the Government for a national policy on better public transport; he was its first Operations Manager. In 1979 he conceived the idea of a "Best Preserved Station" competition, continuing to take an active part, latterly as an Adjudicator, until the end. His books on GWR and LNER passenger carriages remain standard works and he contributed several pieces to the *Oxford Companion to British Railway History*

Right: Michael Harris

5

RESTORATION REWARDED

Above: This timeless view of Oakworth station was taken in 2010, over thirty years after it won the first Awards competition. This wayside station on the Keighley & Worth Valley line has remained in good order over the years, winning other awards and commendations including the Champion's Award in 1989. *Robin Leleux*

of becoming tatty and unappealing. But by the end of the decade this was set to change for the Best Preserved Station Competition was born. Now in 2019 as the National Railway Heritage Awards, it is celebrating its fortieth anniversary.

By 1979 Gordon Biddle was an established author on railway and canal topics, especially on the buildings side, as well as being professionally a land and buildings surveyor, first in local government and then in the insurance business. As such he knew Michael Harris who was working for Ian Allan Ltd and edited that publishing house's *Railway World* magazine. Michael rang Gordon to ask him to come over to discuss one or two thoughts he had had about stations on preserved railways. So their discussion came round to the question what do you think about starting a competition for stations on preserved railways. They roughed out some rules which were then published in *Railway World*. The Association of Railway Preservation Societies under Captain Peter Manisty got wind of this and liked the idea. So the Best Preserved Station Competition was born in the late summer of 1979.

The aims of the competition (set out in the August issue of *Railway World*) have remained largely unchanged over the succeeding forty years, being to encourage the conservation and restoration of old railway buildings which are described as 'any single structure, group of buildings, example of architecture or built environment which has once formed or continues to form part of railway land or premises'. This would include the sympathetic re-use of worthwhile or historic railway structures as part of the wider conservation of the nation's industrial archaeological heritage, an increasingly strong theme of the 1970s. The judges were obviously looking for excellent workmanship and as far as reasonably possible within the entrant's stated aim, authenticity. Other aspects considered were a good life expectancy of the finished

IN THE BEGINNING 1979–1983

As with the Worth Valley line, the Severn Valley Railway's intermediate stations set the standard for buildings restoration in the Awards competition. Arley has also remained much as it was when it was first commended in 1979 and a winner in 1983, winning again in later years. The train is a driving experience special. *Richard Foster*

The third standard setter was the Bluebell Railway, also commended in the first competition of 1979. As the central hub of this long-established heritage railway Horsted Keynes station has been developed over the years but still retains the air of a country junction 35 years later. *Robin Leleux*

7

Restoration Rewarded

Above: As soon as BR was able to submit entries inevitably this included larger stations; Manchester Victoria was among the first to be commended in 1980 and has reappeared in the competition at times since. The destination plaques adorning the frontage tell of past glories for the operating railway. *Robin Leleux*

work, a feeling for 'atmosphere', careful environmental consideration, possible future compatible developments of the site and the potential commercial return for the work by enhancing customer experience. Judging would take place over the next two months without prior notice to prevent artificial tidying up.

Success was immediate, despite the late notice, with eighteen entries being received with a geographical spread from the West Country to the Highlands. Sadly the full list no longer survives (as with certain other early documents which has left a few small holes in our records) but the list of winners does. After much scurrying about the country the handful of judges got together to thrash out the results. These were closely run, such was the initial standard set by the competition entrants, with Oakworth station on the K&WVR emerging the overall winner. It received a handsome inscribed slate plaque which was designed by Alan Breeze who had just previously designed the Eric Treacy memorial plaque at Appleby station. Although not at present on public display at Oakworth station, pending creation of a small museum in the adjacent goods shed,

IN THE BEGINNING 1979–1983

Above: Rowley station was never here, at the site now developed as the Beamish open air museum, but was brought in stone by stone and re-erected. At times looking a bit tired, it was in fine fettle when visited in 2009, almost thirty years after first being entered. *Robin Leleux*

it is brought out on 'high days and holidays'. The five highly commended entries – Arley (Severn Valley Railway), Boat of Garten (Strathspey Railway), Horsted Keynes (Bluebell Railway), Hadlow Road in Wirral Country Park and Middleton Top Engine House – received certificates also designed and prepared by Alan Breeze.

First sponsorship had come from three quarters, Ian Allan Ltd, British Railways, who paid for the winner's plaque, and a small travel agency in Harpenden called Travel Britain Co. Peter Bird, an architect with this firm, joined Gordon, Michael, Bernard Kaukas, BR's Director, Environment, and Marcus Binney, Chairman of the SAVE our heritage campaign as the original band of judges. Although Travel Britain Co received the entries for the 1980 competition, sadly the firm folded and the Association of Railway Preservation Societies (ARPS) had to step in at short notice. It took over the organisation of the competition for several years but it had to be self financing, which is why a £10 entry fee was levied from 1981, becoming £15 by 1990. This was only dropped in 1995 when increasing sponsorship from within the railway industry rendered it unnecessary.

Although ARPS now organised the competition, with Ian Allan Ltd as main sponsor, Peter Manisty let Gordon Biddle and Michael Harris get on with it, with occasional guidance, while he saw to the important background jobs such as keeping up sponsorship and organising the annual awards presentation ceremony. For four successive years he persuaded Sir Peter Parker, the then British Rail Chairman, to do the honours, followed for two years by Robert (later Sir Robert) Reid, his successor. The ceremony was held in rooms at

Restoration Rewarded

Above: Over the years the Mid-Hants Railway has been a constant and successful participant in the Awards competition, winning for the first time with the attractive intermediate station at Ropley in 1981. This too retains its charm (August 2010) despite the inevitable great increase in visitor traffic. *Paul Atterbury*

Euston for three years then at 222 Marylebone Road, the BRB HQ, for another three years.

Precise details of the judging and awarding process in these first years are now lost. For the 1981 competition the judging panel was augmented by the inclusion of David Lloyd of the Victorian Society (which still has its Director on the Panel of Adjudicators), David Pearce, the Secretary of the Society for the Protection of Ancient Buildings, and Tim Cantell, Assistant Secretary, Environment, at the Royal Society of Arts. However, it would appear that assistance with the actual judging was soon required, and in line with Gordon's initial ideas a separate panel would meet after judging was completed to assess all the entries in the light of the judges' marks and reports before adjudicating on the results, a practice which still continues. Early judges included Alan Davies, Richard Horne, John Ives, R. C. (Dick) Riley, Richard Tinker and Duncan Wheeler, most of whom are still on the team. The present writer joined in 1986. A precise judges' marking form was soon devised, supplemented by a written report.

As BR had been involved from the outset with paying for the winner's slate plaque and Bernard Kaukas being one of the judges, it was natural that it should

Above: Highley station has always vied with its neighbour Arley on the Severn Valley Railway for the restoration honours, first winning outright in 1982 and then the Champions Award in 1986.
Robin Leleux

seek to be allowed to enter. So from the next year (1980) a separate class was opened for BR, London Transport and public authority entries although at this stage only Certificates of Commendation were awarded. These first winners were Charlbury (BR [WR]), Edge Hill and Manchester Victoria (both BR [LMR]), and Rowley station in the North of England Open Air Museum at Beamish. Since 1980 BR and London Transport, and their successor companies as the industry has been re-organised, have entered the competition with great enthusiasm; many most important railway structures have now received Awards as they have been restored, refurbished or transformed. Local authorities too have been keen to join in.

The winners of the slate plaque (not yet known as the Premier Award) paid for by BR were Staverton on the Dart Valley Railway (1980), Ropley on the Mid-Hants Railway (a photograph of the unveiling of the plaque in the booking hall there has just come to light, see page 122) (1981) and Highley on the Severn Valley Railway (1982). Arley, Cheddleton (North Staffs Railway), Horsted Keynes and Oakworth all received further commendations in these years; it is fair to say that between them they set the bar high for standards of building restoration in the Awards.

Conversion to Accommodation

Restoration of historic structures is but part of the story; without some form of sustainable reuse, the renovated buildings may simply deteriorate again in the future. One facet of a number of winners and highly commended entries over the years has been conversion to provide some form of accommodation.

Above: The Grade B listed ex-North British Railway signal box at Aberdour – dating originally to 1890 – has been sympathetically converted into an artist's studio after standing redundant for almost 30 years; this was a Highly Commended entry in 2017.
Robert Gardiner

Right: Another ex-North British box to be converted – this time the Grade C listed Currour on the West Highland line – was a winner in 2016. Designed to serve a station built as a hunting lodge for Sir John Stirling-Maxwell, the box, redundant since resignalling of the line in the 1980s has been converted into holiday accommodation. *Gregory Beecroft*

CONVERSION TO ACCOMMODATION

Right: Not all railway buildings are grand; some are purely functional and utilitarian but all have – or had – a role in the operation of the railway. This small structure at Ladybank had, it is believed, originally been the wash house. Over the years the Ladybank Development Trust had undertaken the restoration of much of the historic fabric of this Fife station; its most recent work has seen the conversion of this simple structure into a garden shed. *Gregory Beecroft*

Below: It's not only smaller properties that can be converted into accommodation; in Tavistock the old London & South Western station was restored as a family house and three holiday cottages. It was a justified winner of the *Modern Railways* Restoration Award in 2011. *Michael Papps*

13

CHAPTER 2

A Widening Remit 1983–1989

After four years in which the Awards competition had established itself as an important player in railway heritage, it was time to broaden the remit. *Railway World* for October 1983, in announcing the fifth annual competition, gave the details. Most prominent was the change of name, to The Best Restored Station Competition. There were still two classes of entry but one was broadened: class A, principally for stations of privately preserved lines, could now include stations in other sympathetic use, while class B was for stations still operated by BR, LT or other public authority. This shift in emphasis was important because it widened the scope of the awards from merely acknowledging what was there, albeit nicely presented, to actual restoration and thorough refurbishment work. The article noted that the judges would also be paying particular attention to efforts in creating an attractive public image rather than to 'maintaining strict adherence to a particular historic period'. This pragmatic approach remains a hallmark of the Awards; despite occasional dissension within the Panel of Adjudicators, the Awards have not sought to be a purist architectural competition.

Despite the name, other railway structures had always been accepted. This was clarified in 1984 when it was made clear that any railway (including tramway) structure was eligible. Also individual owners who 'have endeavoured to retain the railway character of their property' were invited to enter. A further innovation was the introduction of First Class Awards as an intermediate level to reflect the increasingly high quality of work being entered which was deserving of something more tangible than a certificate but still below that of the top award. The new awards were in the form of hand painted wooden plaques which, like the overall winner's slate one, were intended to be mounted on the wall. Five were initially awarded, to Bath Green Park (J. Sainsbury plc), Montrose (BR [ScR]) and Saltaire (BR [ER]) in the public sector and Alresford (Mid-Hants Railway) and Blackheath (Blackheath Preservation Trust) in the private. That at Montrose still survives mounted as intended while that for Alresford apparently never arrived.

Two of these winners broke new ground. While Greater Manchester County Council's concurrent conversion of the erstwhile Manchester Central station into the G-Mex concert hall (Manchester Central again since 2007) gave the idea, J. Sainsbury's work in converting the distinctive and locally much loved Bath Green Park station into a supermarket, with the car park under the restored train shed, really showed the way in the sensitive conversion of redundant yet significant stations into new uses; others have triumphantly followed, as will be seen. Such a new use may not even be on the same site, for the wooden station at Lyme

Top: The first wooden First Class Award plaque as presented to Montrose (old) station in 1984. *John Yellowlees*

Above: The first brass Ian Allan Award plaque as presented to Wellingborough station in 1986 *Robin Leleux*

14

A WIDENING REMIT 1983–1989

Above: Distinctive station buildings are an asset to the local townscape and deserve to remain so if operationally redundant but a new use can be found. J. Sainsbury plc showed the way with an excellent conversion of Bath Green Park station into its supermarket in 1984, winning a First Class Award. *Andy Savage*

Regis, dating from the opening of that branch line in 1903 and surviving as a builder's store after closure, was carefully dismantled and carted over to Hampshire to be the new station shop for the Mid-Hants Railway's terminal at Alresford. Again this was the forerunner of other successful schemes on heritage railways, although open-air buildings and industrial museums had already shown the way.

Further innovation came in 1985 when at last the best entry in class B (entries from BR, LT and public authorities) received its own plaque, and the two top awards were named as the Premier Award, still the inscribed slate plaque paid for by BR, and the Ian Allan Award, an etched stainless steel plaque paid for by Ian Allan Ltd. The first winner of this prestigious award was North Woolwich Old Station Museum, restored by the Passmore Edwards Museum Trust aided by the Docklands Development Corporation. Sadly later developments in Docklands necessitated the closure of the museum (the building still stands, woefully abandoned) and dispersal of its records and artifacts. Some went via the Great Eastern Railway Society to the East Anglian Railway Museum at Chappel & Wakes Colne; others probably were transferred from the local authority (the London Borough of Newham) store locally to one in Oxfordshire. The plaque has not surfaced since. However that presented the following year (1986 competition) to the beautifully restored Wellingborough station was in brass and that is still mounted on the wall of the booking hall (page 14). Further winners of the plaque in this period were St Denys (Southampton, BR [SR], 1987), Glasgow

15

RESTORATION REWARDED

Above: The stations on the Midland Railway's Leicester & Hitchen line of 1857 were all similarly designed by C. H. Driver but only that at Wellingborough remains in operational use. Distinctive architectural features are clearly evident following its refurbishment in 1986, shortly before it won the Ian Allan Award. *Robin Leleux*

Below: The impressive station at Lewes has survived despite official suggestions that its canopies be pulled down. A winner of the Ian Allan Award in 1989, it re-appeared in the Awards shortlists in 2017 after much needed refurbishment had been completed.
Robert Thornton

Above: The great curved station at Newcastle, designed by John Dobson (1850) and Thomas Prosser (1863), has been admired, neglected and refurbished piecemeal in turn but in recent years a more concerted programme has resulted in its fine features being properly evident when one walks through these impressive original doors, thanks initially to the late Bernard Kaukas. *Robin Leleux*

Central (Scotrail, 1988) and Lewes (BR [SR], 1989).

Attention to heritage matters was gaining a strong hold within BR during this period. Bernard Kaukas, highly regarded as BR's Chief Architect (1968-1977) was made Director, Environment in 1977. Initially looked down on by Board members, despite his monumental work in persuading BR to spend £3m to prevent St Pancras station's roof from collapsing, he soon made his presence felt! He wanted it known that BR was not neglecting its stock of substantial Victorian buildings, despite lingering indifference to them, and pushed the useful work done at Manchester Victoria, Newcastle, Hull Paragon, Darlington, King's Cross, Liverpool Street and of course St Pancras. He had already become involved with this new competition and links between it and BR were further strengthened when Robert Reid, successor to Sir Peter Parker as BR Chairman, instituted the BR Railway Community Network. Although Bernard retired in 1982, under his enthusiastic colleagues David Perry and James Crowe much useful work was done until the unit was disbanded following rail privatisation a decade later. This included important work at Boston station where the handsome colonnade was fully restored, a project which was Commended in 1993.

At the same time the Railway Heritage Trust was launched in April 1985 under the chairmanship of Sir William McAlpine. Backed by BR but independent of both it and Government, its role was to assist the operational railway in its preservation and upkeep of listed buildings. It was also to facilitate the transfer of non-operational premises and structures to outside bodies willing to undertake their preservation. This is a

Above: Boston received a handsome station in 1848 as befitted its importance as a town sited on the main (albeit short-lived) east coast route to the north. Prominent was the five-arch colonnade welcoming passengers. In 1911 however this was reduced in size and appearance, with the entrance also being moved, to the considerable detriment of the station's appearance. Restoration of the portico to its former size and grace in 1993 was supported by the BR Railway Community Network and received Commendation in the Awards. *Robin Leleux*

significant function, ensuring that valuable railway items were kept and looked after while still in use and when change has removed their operational utility. Its first Executive Director was Leslie Soane who was approaching the end of a highly respected and very senior career in BR, and was of course known to Bernard Kaukas, ultimately joining him as an Adjudicator for the Awards competition. His untimely serious illness early in 1996 necessitated retirement from both positions.

The Railway Heritage Trust became a sponsor for the competition in 1986 with its own named Award – and remains so to the present day – the initial criterion being for the best restored listed building with RHT involvement. A die-cast plaque became the norm. Shrewsbury station (BR [LMR]) became the first winner, followed in 1988 by Great Malvern (BR [WR]), widely known for its richly decorated capitals supporting the platform awnings, in 1988 and Gobowen (BR [LMR] and others) in 1989. (No award was made in 1987.)

Two new stations joined the ranks of Premier Award winners in 1985 and 1986, Bo'ness (Scottish Railway Preservation Society) and Haven Street (Isle of Wight Steam Railway) respectively. Nevertheless, in 1986 and in response to criticism that the same stations were dominating the awards, first as an overall winner and then in the Highly Commended category, a further new award was announced. It was fair comment; Oakworth was, as we have seen, the first overall winner in 1979 and then went on to collect four certificates as did Arley, which won in 1983, while Highley, winner in 1982, also received three certificates. So the Champions Award was instituted for past winners of the Premier Award in the voluntary sector and in its three years was duly won by Highley (1986), Damems, the tiny station between Keighley and Oakworth and winner in 1984, in 1987 and Oakworth in 1989. (No award was made in 1988.)

A further change of name occurred in 1987 with the adoption of The Ian Allan Railway Heritage Awards, reflecting Ian Allan Ltd's considerable input in sponsorship. Indeed without the personal involvement of Ian Allan himself, and in particular over many years of David Allan, the Awards would not have been able to flourish as they have. BR continued to be fully involved with the RHT as third sponsor. As evidence of the increasing standing of the Awards, entry numbers burgeoned: 71 were reported by the closing date of the 1985 competition while the overall record of over 80 was reached in 1989. Precise figures for other years are missing. It was time to widen its appeal as 'Best Restored Station' was seen as too restrictive: the total railway heritage was important. So parts of the station environment and individual features like signal boxes and waiting rooms were welcomed, and while structures like bridges and winding houses had featured in the competition in the past, despite the name, now it was clear that they were eligible; they have performed accordingly.

Further new ground was broken to take advantage of this broader emphasis with successful entries in both 1987 and 1988. While reconstructed buildings had been considered eligible for some time, now there was a place for replica ones, and Kidderminster Town station is a most remarkable example. Built from scratch by the successful Severn Valley Railway on a new site adjacent to the main line station, it is a faithful reproduction of its period prototype, said to be the now-demolished GWR station at Ross-on-Wye. It was a worthy winner of the British Rail Award (formerly the Premier Award) for 1987. Finally successful station restoration is not just the preserve of operational railways, public or heritage, as the Wilkinson Family demonstrated with their magnificent work in bringing Rowden Mill Station in Herefordshire back to life as a private house. Both these paths have since been well trodden again, for example the Churnet Valley Railway's impressive replica North Staffordshire Railway market town station at Kingsley & Froghall (winner in 2005) and fine work by Mr K. R. Mathews at Fencote, just down the line from Rowden Mill, in 1992.

Finally it was clear by 1987 that the competition was not restricted either to the standard gauge railways or to mainland UK, for in that year three winning entries, including one from the Isle of Man, broke the mould, all being Highly Commended. Laxey station on the Isle of Man's Manx Electric Railway stands on a 3ft 0in gauge electrified line at the junction deep inland for the Snaefell Mountain Railway while Dolgoch Falls station stands on the 2ft 3in gauge Talyllyn Railway at

Above and right: Designed by the Oswestry-based architect Thomas Mainwaring Penson for the Shrewsbury & Chester Railway, the neo-Tudor Shrewsbury station was the first recipient of the Railway Heritage Trust Award when the award was instituted in 1986. The first cast plaque was presented by HRH Prince Michael of Kent. *Peter Waller (both)*

Restoration Rewarded

Above: Having developed one of the country's leading heritage railways, and at last arrived back into Kidderminster, the Severn Valley Railway needed an appropriately impressive terminal station. Based on later GWR practice, its new building eminently succeeded and carried off the British Rail Award in 1987. *Robin Leleux*

Below: Less in the public eye than some heritage railways, the Churnet Valley Railway has still managed to build a creditable station at Kingsley & Froghall, the far end of the line, in North Staffordshire Railway style, winning the Ian Allan Publishing Award in 2005. *Robin Leleux*

Above: LUL's first Award came in 1984 when Baker Street was Highly Commended, celebrating the restoration of this iconic original underground station. Originally steam operated, hence the many ventilation shafts, now a modern electric train is approaching. *TfL Visual Services*

the picturesque waterfalls of that name. Moving down yet further in gauge, Llanuwchllyn station lies on the (nominal) 2ft of the Bala Lake Railway on the course of the former BR (WR) Bala and Dolgellau line. Again other such entries have followed.

This period also saw the Awards presentations move away from BRB's offices to other venues, the Royal Society of Arts being used twice, as was Stationers' Hall. Similarly the Guest of Honour was chosen from the wider field of those interested in railways or architecture, David Shepherd the renowned artist, locomotive owner and creator of the heritage railway at Cranmore leading this field in 1986. He was followed by HRH Prince Michael of Kent, the Lord Mayor of London Sir Greville Spratt and Lord Montague of Beaulieu in his capacity as Chairman of English Heritage.

Conversion to Pubs and Cafés

Another reuse of restored railway property – and ideal when the space is part of a still operational station – is conversion into a public house or café. This has two advantages: it gives a practical role for otherwise uneconomic space and it also helps to improve the facilities on offer to the passenger. In many locations, the new pub or café has become a centre of the local community.

Above: When the historic Euston station was demolished in the early 1960s, relatively little of the 19th century station was to survive. Two buildings that did were the small lodges, built some distance south from the main station and slightly later in date. These have both now been successfully converted into small public houses and, following the restoration of their windows – rewarded in 2017 – the buildings now look much as they did externally when they were completed in the 1860s. *John Butler*

CONVERSION TO PUBS AND CAFÉS

Right: One of the most impressive and earliest stations is that in Huddersfield; over the years, however, railway use of the rooms in the main building declined with the result that deterioration set it. The south pavilion was converted into a popular public house some years ago; in 2017 it was the turn of the north pavilion – now the King's Head – to be rewarded. One facet of the work completed here – and so often with these conversions – is the discovery, retention and restoration of period details lost over many years. *Robin Leleux*

Below: Often Network Rail or other property owners will undertake the restoration of a property with no guarantee that a tenant can be found; a case in point was the Grade 2 listed ex-Midland Railway station at Newark. Whilst the fabric of Castle station was restored in 2015, it was not until three years later that a tenant occupied the building, converting it into a café. The new work was Highly Commended in 2018. *John Young*

23

Restoration Rewarded

Right: It's not only the restoration of the building that gets judged; it's the entrants' attention to detail and the finish achieved that also come under the scrutiny of the judges and adjudicators. Chiltern Railways' restoration of the art deco refreshment room on the up platform at Leamington Spa saw the company source the manufacture of replica chairs to those that had originally been supplied in the 1930s.
Edward Dorricott

Left: Over the years Reading station has been enlarged or rebuilt on several occasions with the result that the historic Grade 2 block originally designed by Brunel and remodelled in the 1860s had become increasingly marginalised. For the latest redevelopment, the block has undergone a complete restoration and conversion into the Three Guineas.
Gavin Johns

Right: Another pub conversion that saw the original fabric of the space carefully conserved and restored were the former refreshment rooms at Sheffield station. Constructed in the early 20th century, the rooms had been largely redundant before work commenced in 2009 on converting the Grade 2 listed structure into the Sheffield Tap: a worthy winner of the *Modern Railways* Restoration Award in 2010.
Railway Heritage Trust

CONVERSION TO PUBS AND CAFÉS

Right: It is not only major towns and cities that have benefited from this type of conversion; the ex-Highland Railway station at Tain became virtually derelict after it became unmanned in 1991. More than two decades later the building was restored and reopened as the Platform 1864 restaurant. *Gavin Johns*

Below: In the early 20th century tea rooms were built to serve York station; when these closed, the space was used for a variety of functions – including, for a period, the housing of a model railway – until work started in 2011 on its conversion to a public house – the York Tap. The work involved the complete refurbishment of the exterior and the reinstatement of the revolving door casing. *Deborah Trebinski*

25

CHAPTER 3

Using the Past to Serve the Future 1989–1994

The Ian Allan Railway Heritage Awards, now under its third name, was well set to enter its second decade in 1989. Ian Allan Ltd was substantially the main sponsor, aided enthusiastically by BR with its Railway Community Link and by the Railway Heritage Trust. ARPS, under the energetic leadership of Peter Manisty, continued to run the competition but he was content to let 'Biddle's Boys' as he called them get on with it. ARPS members like Arthur Harding, who played a background role in the Awards administration for some years, received the entries and organised the judging. However, by 1991, problems were arising in this respect as ARPS nominees juggled their work and own heritage railway commitments so Gordon Biddle asked Robin Leleux, who was neither a railwayman nor associated with ARPS but a published railway historian, to take over (he cannot now remember why he made this choice but it certainly worked out as Robin ran the judging for the next twenty years before moving to chair the Panel of Adjudicators). An early task was first to weed the list of judges (unfortunately some were not that effective) and then to strengthen it nationwide, so that it comprised railwaymen, architects, surveyors, authors and indeed any interested person who 'could view a building sensibly with open eyes'.

Sponsorship was also beginning gradually to widen, with British Coal joining in from 1988 with a cash prize of £100. First winner was Oakworth booking hall with its signature welcoming coal fire, followed in 1989 by the restoration of Radstock North signal box at Didcot by the Great Western Society. Then came the first Westinghouse Best Restored Signalling Award as a new, specific award to recognise the growing work undertaken by heritage railways in restoring their mechanical signalling heritage. This was first won in 1992 by the Severn Valley Railway's impressive new signalling at Kidderminster; it received a die-cast metal plaque and a cheque for £250. Under various names, reflecting the ownership of Westinghouse Brake & Signal Ltd, this award remained an important feature of the annual competition. The next two winners were Muston signal box, York, of the Great Yorkshire Railway Preservation Society, and Exeter West signal box at Crewe Heritage Centre of the Exeter West Group.

Probably the most significant organisational change in this period was moving the entire Awards competition process into the one calendar year. This meant an earlier call for entries, by the end of May, judging to be organised in June and completed by the end of August, adjudication during September and the Awards Presentation Ceremony in early December, rather than doing the judging in the autumn and holding the Awards Presentation Ceremony in the early spring of the following year. By the time Gordon and Robin had determined this, not long after the March 1991 ceremony for the 1990 Awards, there was no time

Right: The impressive new Kidderminster Station signal box was the first winner of the new Westinghouse Best Restored Signalling Award in 1992. A substantial box in later GWR style, it is needed to control the complex signalling at this busy terminus of the Severn Valley Railway. *Robin Leleux*

Above: In 1989 the Keighley & Worth Valley Railway added to its station stock by rebuilding the former station at Ingrow with the building from Foulridge, near Colne and also of Midland Railway parentage, so winning the British Rail Premier Award.
Robin Leleux

Right: The British Rail Premier Award was not confined to stations, being won by this fine reconstruction of the ornate Bowes Lyon Bridge over the tramway at Crich Tramway Village in 1992.
Robin Leleux

to organise a competition for that year. So no awards were made for 1991 and the competition was re-launched in spring 1992. Stationers' Hall, Glaziers' Hall and the Royal Society of Arts were the ceremony venues, with Sir Robert Reid (as he now was) and Bob Reid, his successor at BRB, HRH the Duke of Gloucester and the Lord Mayor of London Christopher Walford variously doing the honours as principal guest.

RESTORATION REWARDED

Above: The deterioration of the iconic Ribblehead Viaduct was a *cause célèbre* when the future of the Settle & Carlisle line was under intense scrutiny, so its repair, following the line's celebrated reprieve, justly brought it the Ian Allan Award in 1993. A Class 158 DMU crosses under a snow-clad Whernside, illustrating the bleakness of the location. *Robin Leleux*

Right: The restoration of the impressive harbourside station at Wemyss Bay, near Glasgow, was justly celebrated – a picture of its clock tower made the national press – and won for it the Ian Allan Award in 1994. Its subsequent decay under successive indifferent administrations was cause for concern, so its second great rejuvenation over twenty years later was equally welcome, winning the Best Overall Entry for 2017 (see also page 99). *via Andy Savage*

28

Using the Past to Serve the Future 1989–1994

A new Award from 1990 was the *Railway World* Commendation for nearly complete projects in the voluntary sector. The first winner was Grosmont station, always a busy one on the North Yorkshire Moors Railway, in 1991. 'K4' Class No 61994 *The Great Marquess* stands ready to leave on an up train. *Robin Leleux*

Above: In time the Bluebell Railway was able to begin its long-desired extension northwards. Kingscote was its first destination, the station here winning the *Railway World* Award in 1992 not long before its final opening. Ten years later the quality of restoration is still well evident. *Robin Leleux*

Restoration Rewarded

Above: The Mid-Suffolk Light Railway was a never completed venture in rural East Anglia but its memory lingered long after closure in 1952, prompting enthusiasts to resurrect its memory at Brockford station. Here surviving buildings from other intermediate stations were collected, and a distinctively ornate 'Middy' nameboard re-created. This won the *Railway World* Award in 1994. *Robin Leleux*

The title of this chapter is cribbed from that used by Gordon Biddle in a commemorative pull-out for *Railway World* in 1999, celebrating twenty years of the Awards, but it is relevant at this stage of the story. The broadening scope of the Awards, as detailed earlier, was rewarded by a yet wider spectrum of entrants and winners. The usual entry lists from regions of BR, BRB regional architects and its Property Board, London Transport and established heritage railways were joined by local authorities, brewers, museums, private practices of architects and surveyors, trusts caring for restored stations, often converted to other private use, and private individuals. This is reflected in the range of winners of the British Rail Premier Award for the voluntary sector, being Ingrow (K&WVR – the station building from Foulridge being re-erected on this new site in the Keighley suburbs) in 1989, Errol (Errol Station Trust, Perthshire) in 1990, the Bowes Lyon Bridge at Crich (Tramway Museum Society) in 1992, Scotscalder Station house in Caithness by Daniel Brittain-Catlin in 1993 and the new station building at Cranmore, East Somerset Railway, in 1994. The Ian Allan Award, as the premier award for the public sector, also had an interesting range, being Lewes station (1989), the Wicker Arch (site of Sheffield's first station) in 1990, the Cathedral Arches in Salford (BR Property Board) in 1992, Ribblehead Viaduct (this did not please David Allan, who preferred a station to win the award his company sponsored, despite this iconic structure being treasured by Yorkshire people everywhere) in 1993, and Wemyss Bay station in Strathclyde (David Allan vindicated!) in 1994.

Two new awards appeared in this period. The *Railway World* Commendation (its name varied over the years) began in 1990 and was awarded to the best voluntary sector project nearing completion. A cash prize of £1,000 came with it, along with a die-cast

Above: Worksop station was originally designed by James Drabble for the Manchester, Sheffield & Lincolnshire Railway in 1849, being extended fifty years later by the Great Central Railway. This solid building was nicely restored in 1990 to win the Railway Heritage Trust Award, and to win again in 2018. *Bill Free*

plaque, presented by Ian Allan Ltd. Also in the voluntary sector, recognising work solely done by volunteers, was the Worth Valley Award, also a plaque, presented by the K&WVR from 1992. Notable winners of these were Grosmont station (North Yorkshire Moors Railway), Kingscote station (Bluebell Railway), Isfield station (Lavender Line in East Sussex) and tiny Brockford station (Mid-Suffolk Light Railway Society) for the incomplete schemes and Littlehempston (South Devon Railway) and Kingswear stations (Dart Valley Light Railway) for the totally volunteer projects. In a modified and amalgamated form these awards survive.

Other notable award winners in this period included Gobowen station, on the Welsh borders near Oswestry, which had been revived under some pressure and considerable involvement by senior pupils of a local school (BR [LMR] and others, RHT Award 1989); other RHT Award winners were Worksop (BR Regional Civil Engineer, York, 1990) and the distinctively tiled North Staffordshire Railway station roof at Stoke-on-Trent, its main station (BR Property Board 1993). The East Lancashire Railway, then a relative newcomer on the heritage railway scene, triumphed in two successive years with First Class Awards for its new stations at Rawtenstall (1992) and Ramsbottom (1993), while the Welshpool & Llanfair Railway similarly won with its new Raven Square Station at Welshpool, using the old station building from Eardisley in Herefordshire (1992). London Underground renewed its winning ways in 1993 with First Class Awards for Chesham and Gloucester Road stations, while Ireland first entered the lists in 1992.

Initially Irish entries, from either side of the border, were handled by John Lockett, the ARPS Chairman in Ireland. He recruited two Irish Railway Record Society

RESTORATION REWARDED

(IRRS) members with civil engineering and architecture backgrounds as judges. Seven entries were received that year, with the Ardglass & Downpatrick Railway winning a First Class Award with Downpatrick station and Iarnród Éireann (IE) was Highly Commended for work at Malahide in Co Dublin. Unfortunately problems arose, such that the judging results for the 1993 entries were not notified through until well into 1994 when Bagenalstown station (IE) was highly commended.

Sadly Peter Manisty died in 1992, to be succeeded as the Chairman of ARPS by his deputy, David Morgan, a London solicitor. A management committee

Left: Stoke-on-Trent station is an integral part of Winton Square so its restoration in the early 1990s, especially the decorative roof with its distinctive bands of red tiles amid the blue, was important and welcomed. It won the Railway Heritage Trust Award in 1993. *RHT*

Below: The East Lancashire Railway may have been a relative newcomer on the heritage railway scene but quickly established itself, not least with two new build stations replacing those previously lost. Ramsbottom won a First Class Award in 1993. *Deborah Trebinski*

32

Above: Chesham remains a distant outpost of London Underground's Metropolitan Line, having been built by the erstwhile Metropolitan Railway in 1889. Its refurbishment in 1993 won a First Class Award for LUL. *Robin Leleux*

Below: In 1993 LUL won double, for Gloucester Road also received a First Class Award. This is really a twin station, for the prominent Piccadilly Line part, with its characteristic red tiled facade by Leslie Green of 1906, stands alongside the much earlier (1868) District and Circle Line building to the right. *Robin Leleux*

Restoration Rewarded

was formed, initially meeting in David Morgan's offices in Gray's Inn, but then round the corner in a convenient hostelry.

Various people had been brought in by 1995 to broaden the effectiveness of the committee. Gordon already knew David Lawrence, Director of the BR Property Board, through his association with the Northern Viaducts Trust – its Smardale Gill viaduct in Cumbria won a First Class Award in 1992 – so despite earlier differences in approach between the Property Board and the Director, Environment, he brought David in as Awards Manager. He also brought in Peter Fells as Treasurer, as more money was being handled. ARPS suggested Peter Thomas from the Bluebell Railway who took over from David as Awards Manager, along with Arthur Harding. David Allan also regularly attended. Unfortunately the minutes for this period have not surfaced so more precise dating has not been possible.

Peter Manisty's contribution to the success of the Awards is unsung because it was largely behind the scenes. However, as a tribute to him at the 1993 ceremony a major award was named in his honour, the Peter Manisty Award for Excellence. This was not to be an annual occurrence but only given when a really outstanding entry deserved it. The refurbishment of the great London terminal station at Liverpool Street was a worthy winner, its reconstruction and remodelling including two new frontage towers designed to blend in with the adjacent old ones; its entry into the Awards demonstrated how important they were now perceived to be. Other highly prestigious projects have followed where BR at Liverpool Street has led.

Left: A view of the much admired west-side low-numbered platform concourse at Liverpool Street, created as part of the 1991 station. All the building in the picture including the roof is 1980s build designed by Nick Derbyshire. Gordon Biddle called it 20th century Victorian Gothic Revival. *Theo Steel*

Bridges and Tunnels

Abandoned bridges and tunnels pose a challenge if they are to be preserved; increasingly reuse is found in the creation of new cycle paths and redundant railway routes now play a significant part of the growing National Cycle Network. On operational railways there is often the problem as to how historic elements can be integrated into modern structures capable of dealing with contemporary traffic.

Above: Combe Tunnel – to the south of Bath on the former Somerset & Dorset route – is an example of a successful conversion of a tunnel to form part of a cycleway.
Robert Medland

BRIDGES AND TUNNELS

Above: Landowners could often demand that the railway companies go to great lengths to disguise the presence of the railways crossing their land. One classic case was at Gisburn, between Blackburn and Hellifield, where to avoid causing distress to the owner's horses, the Lancashire & Yorkshire Railway built an unnecessary tunnel that they completed with castle-like portals. Over the years the condition of the tunnel deteriorated, so much so that a tree was found growing through the stonework. A complex restoration project saw the portals refurbished and the structure returned to a safe condition. *Robin Leleux*

Right: Over the years a considerable amount of work has been undertaken on the LB&SCR station at Lewes; in 2015 attention turned to the late 19th century road overbridge both to refurbish the structure but also – and more importantly – to strengthen it to cater for the ever-increasing weight of traffic. The resulting work saw the strengthening successfully integrated within the original bridge and thus having no impact visually. *Theo Steel*

37

RESTORATION REWARDED

Left: When confronted by the need to upgrade the bridge across the River Witham in Lincoln, the engineers were faced by the challenge of trying to incorporate the listed tubular box edge girders first installed when the bridge was built by John Fowler for the Manchester, Sheffield & Lincolnshire Railway. The original girders were carefully restored and integrated into the design of the new bridge with the paintwork – light grey and green – being adopted to differentiate between the old and new work respectively.
Bill Free

Above: The five-arch wrought-iron viaduct at Ouseburn, which replaced an earlier timber structure in 1869 and was widened in 1885, is now Grade 2* listed; this was to win the Ian Allan Publishing Award in 2013 as the best overall entry that year. The work saw the strengthening of the structure and, as a result, it was possible to raise the line speed over it whilst retaining all its historic features. *Duncan Wheeler*

BRIDGES AND TUNNELS

Above: As the railway preservation movement gets more ambitious, so the work undertaken gets more complex. For the planned restoration of services between Robertsbridge and Bodiam, on the Kent & East Sussex Railway, the Rother Valley Railway has constructed a number of replacement bridges; these were shortlisted in 2013. *Robert Hayward*

Below: The work of converting a disused bridge or viaduct into a cycleway can be extensive; it often involves the creation of a new surface and the provision of barriers on either side of the path. This example is Tuckingmill viaduct, south of Bath, on the former Somerset & Dorset line. *Robert Medland*

RESTORATION REWARDED

Above: It is a sobering fact that some lines and structures have now been in preservation for more than half a century and so preservation itself faces the challenge of restoring its own structures. A case in point was the 1854 bridge at Tan-y-Bwlch, which was Highly Commended in 2017 after a major restoration scheme. *Alan Norton/Ffestiniog Railway*

Bridges and Tunnels

CHAPTER 4

Towards Independence 1995–1999

The later 1990s turned out to be a crucial period in the development of the Awards as a free-standing organisation widely respected by the railway industry; in 2004 it finally emerged as an independent self-governing charity. The first step along this long road was to change the name in 1995 for the fourth time, becoming the National Railway Heritage Awards (NRHA), although 'Ian Allan' remained as part of the title in the Call for Entries brochure until 2001.

At the same time change was afoot in ARPS. This had emerged as the umbrella organisation – the 'Trade Association' as David Morgan described it – for the railway heritage sector. There was also the Association of Minor Railway Companies which had changed its name to the Association of Independent Railways (AIR) in 1988. The Report written by David Lawrence in 1995 recommended that these two organisations merge which they did as the Association of Independent Railways and Preservation Societies (AIRPS) in 1996. (It took its present name as the Heritage Railway Association Ltd –

Mike Stanbury

Mike had an early introduction to railways: his mother worked in the Shareholders Office of the LNWR, and later the LMS. Mike spent 28 years as a police officer, and is also a family man, with two sons, but he has made a massive contribution to the heritage rail movement. His first office was Treasurer of the South East Essex Railway Society, from age 17 to 21. He joined the embryo Stour Valley Railway Preservation Society in 1968, and has been a member ever since, currently being both the Secretary and a Trustee, plus a Director of the trading company. Mike was instrumental in the railway gaining charitable status, as the East Anglian Railway Museum, in 1991. He then used this experience to help the Mid Suffolk Railway and the LNER Coach Association follow suit. Mike has been a Friend of Fedecrail since 1979, and a Life Member of the Heritage Railway Association since 1990. He joined the NRHA in 1990 as Treasurer, becoming Secretary in 1992, and was a key leader in the Awards gaining charitable status in 2004.

Right: Mike Stanbury. *Duncan Phillips/NRHA*
Above: Award plaque. *Paul Pascoe*

Above: The fine Midland Station at Nottingham was designed by A. E. Lambert in 1904; faced with red sandstone and ornate terracotta, it was designed to rival the GCR's and GNR's new Victoria station in the city. Various refurbishments in recent years have kept it looking smart. This view was taken prior to the recent fire at the station. *Keith Hodgkins*

HRA – in 1998.) David Morgan was Chairman. Increasingly the perception grew that the new organisation was too preoccupied with the business of organising and promoting heritage railways – inevitably given how extensively this field was expanding, especially in the burgeoning tourist industry – to be much bothered with running a heritage buildings competition. NRHA came to feel a long way down the scale of importance.

An important change had occurred at the Railway Heritage Trust, for early in 1996 Leslie Soane fell seriously ill and resigned from 31 March. His successor as Executive Director was Jim Cornell, fresh from a very senior career on BR, who was to prove a very good friend and supporter of the Awards. With a new chairman needed, David Morgan having stood down, he came up with 'I have just the man for you' in John Ellis, also fresh from a very senior career in BR. This was an inspired choice for John has guided the organisation expertly for more than twenty years now. Precise dates for these changes are now lacking but suffice it to say that by 1999 committee meetings were being held in McAlpine's offices, courtesy of Sir William, Chairman of RHT. Subsequently, thanks to Elsa Redpath, Virgin Trains assisted with providing accommodation for these at Euston, before finally Network Rail allowed an office to be booked at its Eversholt Street complex round the corner.

As Awards Manager, Peter Thomas brought in Mike Stanbury from ARPS as Treasurer after Peter Fells left. Mike subsequently preferred to move across as Secretary, being replaced as Treasurer by Tony Tomkins from the Leighton Buzzard Light Railway. Sadly Peter collapsed and died suddenly, his role being then filled by Richard Tinker who had been appointed Company Secretary and assistant to Leslie Soane at the RHT, remaining thus with Jim Cornell. Meanwhile the Awards continued unperturbed. A thin year in 1994 (at 28 entries the lowest figure since 1981) was followed by two strong years of over 50 entries each. The presentation ceremony seemed well placed at the Royal Institute of British Architects (RIBA); an attempt to move out of London was not a success, despite being at the National Railway Museum (1997). Stationers' Hall was the other venue again. The Guests of Honour included Chris Green, by then Chief Executive of English Heritage, John Swift QC, the Rail Regulator, James Sherwood, the President of Sea Containers Ltd, Glenda Jackson, the actress turned politician and at the time Minister of Transport, and Clive Martin, the Lord Mayor of London.

RESTORATION REWARDED

The imperturbability of the Awards competition did come as a surprise to observers, bearing in mind the wholesale privatisation of the national rail industry from 1994, and all credit to both the Management Committee and entrants throughout the railway industry for keeping it so. Michael Harris wrote in *Railway World* (January 1996) that fears that this might seriously reduce the number of entrants for the 1995 competition had proved unfounded. Rather the reverse had been true as there now existed a wider number of agencies within the industry to put forward entries. The entry fee had been dropped as increasing sponsorship made it unnecessary. This was indeed a welcome development for the future health of the competition and its increasing standing with those responsible for the conservation of the UK's railway heritage.

Above: The winner of the Ian Allan Award in 1998 was Aviemore station, unusual in being a joint entry between Railtrack and the Strathspey Railway, the latter being able to run into dedicated platforms just to the right. *NRHA*

Michael Harris went on to make three points which remain most pertinent to entrants and judges today. He warned against entrants focusing their restoration and then their entry submission too closely onto one historic period which might ultimately be impossible fully to achieve because of other present factors, such as colour lighting or corporate signage and livery. Memories of Network South East red lampposts all over London and the south-east were still fresh! That is not to say that the house liveries of franchised train operators were necessarily any more suitable. He then said that they should beware of false heritage ornaments such as 'off-the-shelf' cast-iron bollards, false awnings and an 'olde worlde' atmosphere in tea rooms: less can be more. But he also stressed the importance of operational practicality, especially with an eye open for vandalism.

Left: Another award winning station on the Keighley & Worth Valley railway is tiny Damems whose platform is barely one coach long. Attractively sited by a steep lane and guarded by a level crossing, it collected the last British Rail Award in 1995. *Robin Leleux*

Towards Independence 1995–1999

With the demise of BR, its named award reverted to the Premier Award; the first winner in 1997 was Dunster station, the stop before Minehead on the West Somerset Railway. *NRHA*

Levisham station on the North Yorkshire Moors Railway is a long way from its village but is an important crossing point for trains. Its small station buildings remain sufficient for available traffic with several awards coming its way including the Ian Allan Award in 1999 'B1' class No 61264 stands ready to leave for Grosmont. *Robin Leleux*

RESTORATION REWARDED

Above: The Duke of Sutherland built this part of the Far North railway here and had his own station at the entrance to his castle: Dunrobin station, rebuilt in 1902 in this form. It varied between private, for his lordship's personal use, and public by agreement. After re-opening in 1985 it was attractively restored by Daniel Brittain-Catlin, winning the Premier Award in 1998. *NRHA*

Two new sponsors joined in 1995. The Railtrack Award recognised the best restored Railtrack station by a third party with a plaque and cheque for £1,000 while London Underground, already a regular entrant and winner, instituted an award for the best restored urban commuter station (again a plaque and cheque for £1,000). The first winners were Wymondham station in Norfolk (Mr David Turner) and Whitehead station in Co Antrim (Northern Ireland Railways and Design II Architects) respectively. That brought the total of plaques awarded to eight, a figure which has only slightly increased since. The main winners' plaques were still the inscribed brass (public sector) and gilded slate (voluntary sector) and remained so for some more years yet. Their winners included in the public sector Nottingham station booking hall, the Platform Gallery (the former Clitheroe station) and Aviemore station in Scotland, a joint winning entry between Railtrack and the Strathspey Railway; in the voluntary sector (the name reverted to 'Premier Award' in 1997 with the demise of BR) were tiny Damems station on the K&WVR, the Station House restaurant at Ilderton in Northumberland, Dunster station and goods shed on the West Somerset Railway, buildings at Levisham station on the North Yorkshire Moors Railway, and another fine offering from Daniel Brittain-Catlin, this time Dunrobin Castle station in distant Sutherland.

A very significant winner of the Ian Allan Award (the main public and commercial sector one) in 1997 was the redevelopment of St Marks station in Lincoln into a shopping centre. Lincoln had been the less than willing recipient of two adjacent stations by 1848, each with their own level crossing over the main road into the city, the Midland Railway's serving the Nottingham line and the Great Northern Railway's serving everywhere else. Nearly thirty years after BR was created, it finally did something to alleviate the problem by building a connecting spur from the ex-MR/LMS line into the ex-GNR/LNER system and running all

Above: The Railway Heritage Trust Award went to three very different winners in successive years. In 1995 the grand station at Bury St Edmunds, 'one of the finest in Eastern England' (Biddle) took the honours. Probably designed by Sancton Wood in 1847, it is built in red brick with stone dressings and boasts two domed baroque towers. *NRHA*

Nottingham line trains into the now named Central Station, allowing the MR/LMS one (later St Marks) to be closed. But it had a fine classical frontage which was imaginatively incorporated into the retail development, although building a new department store so close opposite did spoil the effect somewhat. This award was renamed the Ian Allan Publishing Award in 1998, then the *Modern Railways* Award in 1999, but no longer with a brass plaque. Skipton station was the first recipient of the renamed award.

There were several other significant winners to note. For three successive years the RHT Award went to a succession of very different entries, beginning with the partial restoration of the grand station at Bury St Edmunds (1995, BR Property Board and Nick Derbyshire Design Associates). In 1996 by contrast came the tiny wayside station of Humberstone Road, Leicester, removed stone by stone by Leicestershire County Council to form the new Shenton station on the Battlefield Line. Different again was the lofty Lambley Viaduct over the Tyne in Northumberland (1997, BR Property Board again). The London Underground Award for an urban station varyingly went to Braintree, Blackburn, (1996, 1998, both Railtrack) and Barons Court (1997, LUL) and finally to the grand 1938 LMS-build North Concourse at Leeds, newly opened up (1999 Teesland Group plc with Railtrack). The restored station at Corfe Castle on the Swanage Railway, and the rebuilt station at Bolton Abbey on the Embsay Steam Railway both received the Railway World Commendation (1996,1995) but perhaps the most unusual recipient of this award was St Saviour's Church at Swanwick Junction at the Midland Railway Centre in 1998, a 'tin tabernacle' removed from near Westhouses MPD once its mission there had ended.

The Peter Manisty Award for Excellence was again awarded to an outstanding entry, this time in 1995, the recipient being the BR Property Board in association

Above: The second of the trio and 1996 winner began life as the humble Humberstone Road Halt on the outskirts of Leicester. Long after closure it was removed, courtesy of Leicestershire County Council, to serve the new country park at Shenton at the southern end of the Battlefield Line. (The name commemorates the Battle of Bosworth fought nearby in 1483.) *Robin Leleux*

Above: The cover of the brochure for the 1997 Awards Competition, showing the north portal of Clayton Tunnel on the Brighton line. *Robin Leleux*

with The Conservation Practice and Margaret & Richard Davies & Associates for the stunning restoration of the exterior of the great former Midland Hotel at St Pancras, which many people of course think of as being 'St Pancras station'. The attention to detail over such an extensive frontage (both in width and height) was superb, presaging more far-reaching developments to come in the next decade. But this was not the end, for the murals and painted ceiling, lovingly (or extravagantly, according to taste) commissioned by the Midland Railway to adorn its magnificent Grand Staircase, were also fully restored

Irish entries came in regularly from IE, NIR and various heritage railway sites, Millstreet station in Co Cork being Commended in 1996, Whitehead's success having already been mentioned. By this time the judging team there needed overhaul; with the help of John Lockett two keen judges from Northern Ireland were recruited in Douglas Ferguson and Derek Young, the latter having become known to the Chairman of the Judges (as he was by then described) from a chance meeting on the steps of Bangor (Co Down) signal box one evening.

During his time as Awards Manager David Lawrence introduced the regular 'Call for Entries' brochure. This was based on an experimental one put out in 1994 and featuring in a photographic montage a picture of Daniel Brittain-Catlin smilingly holding his winner's slate plaque for Scotscalder station. That for 1995 was A5 size and featured Wemyss Bay station, the previous year's winner. Matters settled down for the 1997 competition at A4 size with a full colour photograph on the front and definitive text within, concluding with a list of awards and sponsors on the rear. A paper entry form was enclosed. The first subject was the distinctive portal of Clayton Tunnel, on the Brighton Line, with its historic 'policeman's' (i.e. signaller's) cottage above. This was followed by Meldon Viaduct (1998) and the replica heritage lamps at Horton-in-Ribblesdale on the Settle & Carlisle (part of the determined effort to emphasise that line's heritage following its reprieve from closure). Creating the brochure was always an interesting exercise: Robin Leleux would take the boxes of the current year's judging slides down to Jonathan Bingham at Ian Allan Printing. There they would tip them out onto a light box and whittle the collection down to a few possibles, the criteria being eye-catching, preferably public sector (to attract busy managers who might immediately bin a heritage one as irrelevant), and able to fit a portrait orientation. Matters got easier with the advent of digital photography …

Right: Illustrating the wide variety of architectural and historical detail to be found on London Underground's stations, Barons Court boasts a balustrade and broken pediment as well as the name of its original railway owner. It won the London Underground Award in 1997. *Robin Leleux*

Robin Leleux

Having been a history master for several years Robin Leleux moved into personnel work with one of the teaching unions. However he maintained his lifelong interest in railways and history by giving talks, teaching WEA classes and leading U3A groups. He wrote the *East Midlands* volume in the David & Charles *Regional Railway Histories* series and also contributed several items to the *Oxford Companion to British Railway History*. In 1991 he established his management consultancy and also took on organising the Awards judging for the next twenty years, having joined the team five years earlier. He was one of the original trustees when the Awards became a charity in 2004 and became Chairman of the Panel of Adjudicators in 2012.

Right: Robin Leleux. *Duncan Phillips/NRHA*

Above: The lofty and slender Lambley Viaduct was the third winner of this trio (1997). Situated mid-way along the former Alston branch on the Cumbria/Northumberland border, it crosses the River South Tyne. Dating from 1852, its railway was closed in 1976 and while pedestrians can cross, there is no onward path at the southern end. *Robin Leleux*

In *Railway World* for January 1997 Michael Harris wrote that the railway scene was so different now than when the Awards were launched in 1979, both in the 'national scene' and with heritage railways. The scale of restorations, to other railway buildings as well as stations, would not have seemed possible then. Many owners spend considerable effort in time and money on their historic buildings, now often with support from public bodies and commercial sponsors. He continued that the Awards' overall principles had not changed from the outset: to promote careful design and quality workmanship in restoration, modernisation and maintenance, bearing in mind too factors like available finance and manpower. The ultimate end is to present the operator's premises, whether public or heritage, as an attractive 'shop window'.

He then emphasised that another continuing aim of the Awards was to present great achievements of restoration country-wide to a wider audience, including where this had involved the conversion of former railway buildings to other uses. So there was a commercial motivation too driving work which in turn both pushed higher standards of restoration and further stimulated the search for new uses for redundant railway buildings, especially where otherwise costs would not justify restoration. Gordon Biddle likewise emphasised these points in his 1999 *Railway World* retrospective supplement, stating that in 1983 there were about 600 railway buildings in Britain statutorily scheduled or listed, which many felt was a lot; now (1999) there were some 1,700, which speaks for itself. Likewise over 750 entries had been received for the awards competition over the past twenty years. He concluded: 'We believe that, properly maintained and managed, these important elements of the country's industrial heritage can serve a dual role in a dynamic railway industry by interpreting the past for the benefit and service of the future, with the emphasis on service.'

So the Awards moved into the new millennium in good heart, with a strong mission and an active management to achieve it.

Above and below: The railway history of Leeds is more complex than today's single extensive station might suggest. Its distinctive North concourse, linking the main concourse with the direct exit to City Square through a rotunda, dates from 1938 and was designed by W. H. Hamlyn, the LMS chief architect, to link two stations. Its reinforced concrete structure anticipated the post-war Portal frame; fortunately its elegant features survived the ignominy of becoming a shabby car park until splendidly restored in 1999. It won the London Underground Award. *Robin Leleux (both)*

RESTORATION REWARDED

Left: 'Tin tabernacles' as they were popularly known were easily erected for churches to minister to new or scattered congregations, such as that for the Midland Railway workers and their families at the locomotive depot and yards at Westhouses in rural Derbyshire. After depot and yards closed the now-redundant St Saviour's Church with its strong railway connections was moved to the Midland Railway Centre for safe keeping, earning the *Railway World* Award for doing so. *Robin Leleux*

Below and right: In the 1990s work was done on a lesser known aspect of the Midland Hotel, the murals, painted ceiling and Grand Staircase within. The latter can be appreciated by patrons moving from the bar by Euston Road to the main foyer and Reception area. This important project justifiably won the prestigious Peter Manisty Award for Excellence in 1995. *Robin Leleux*

52

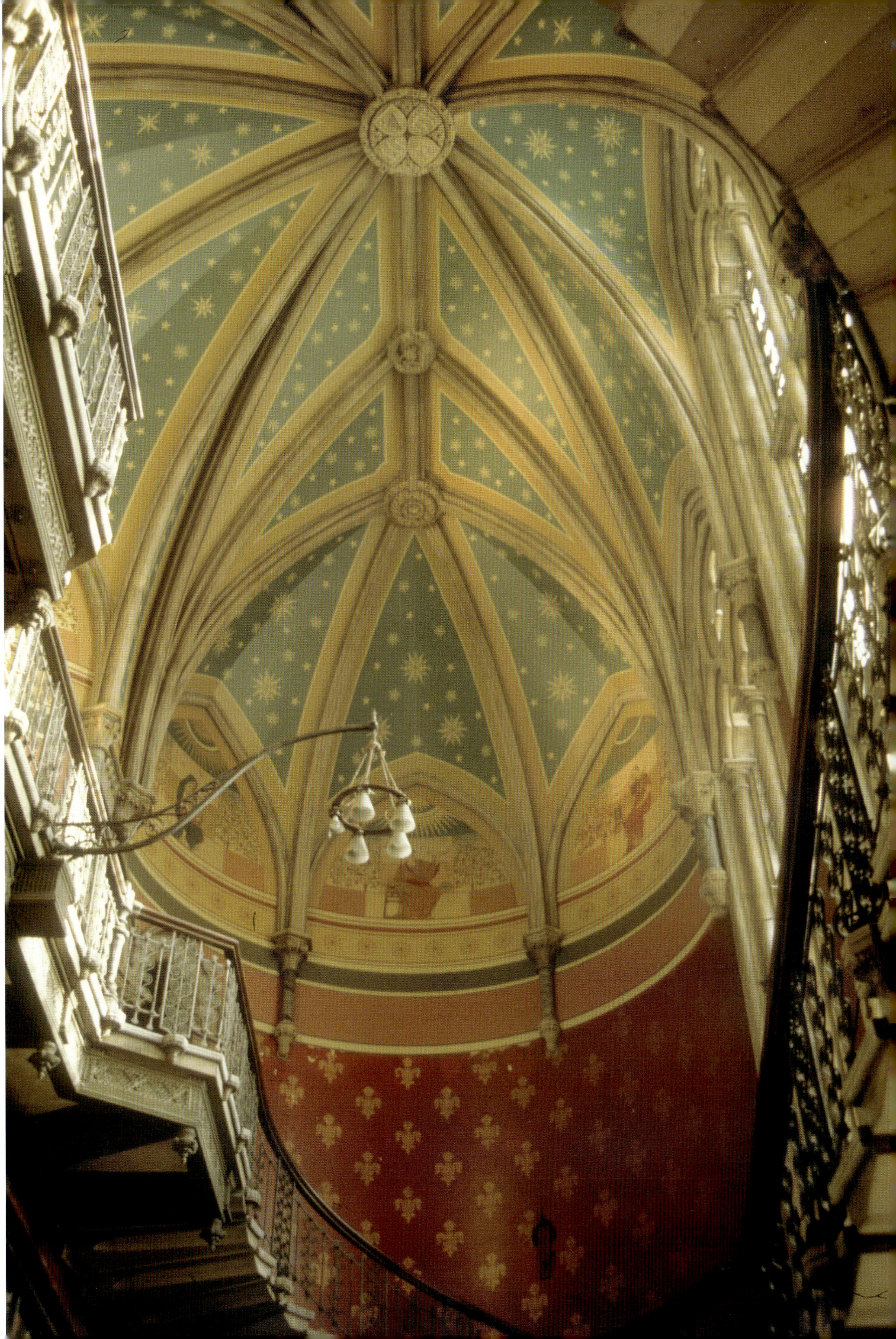

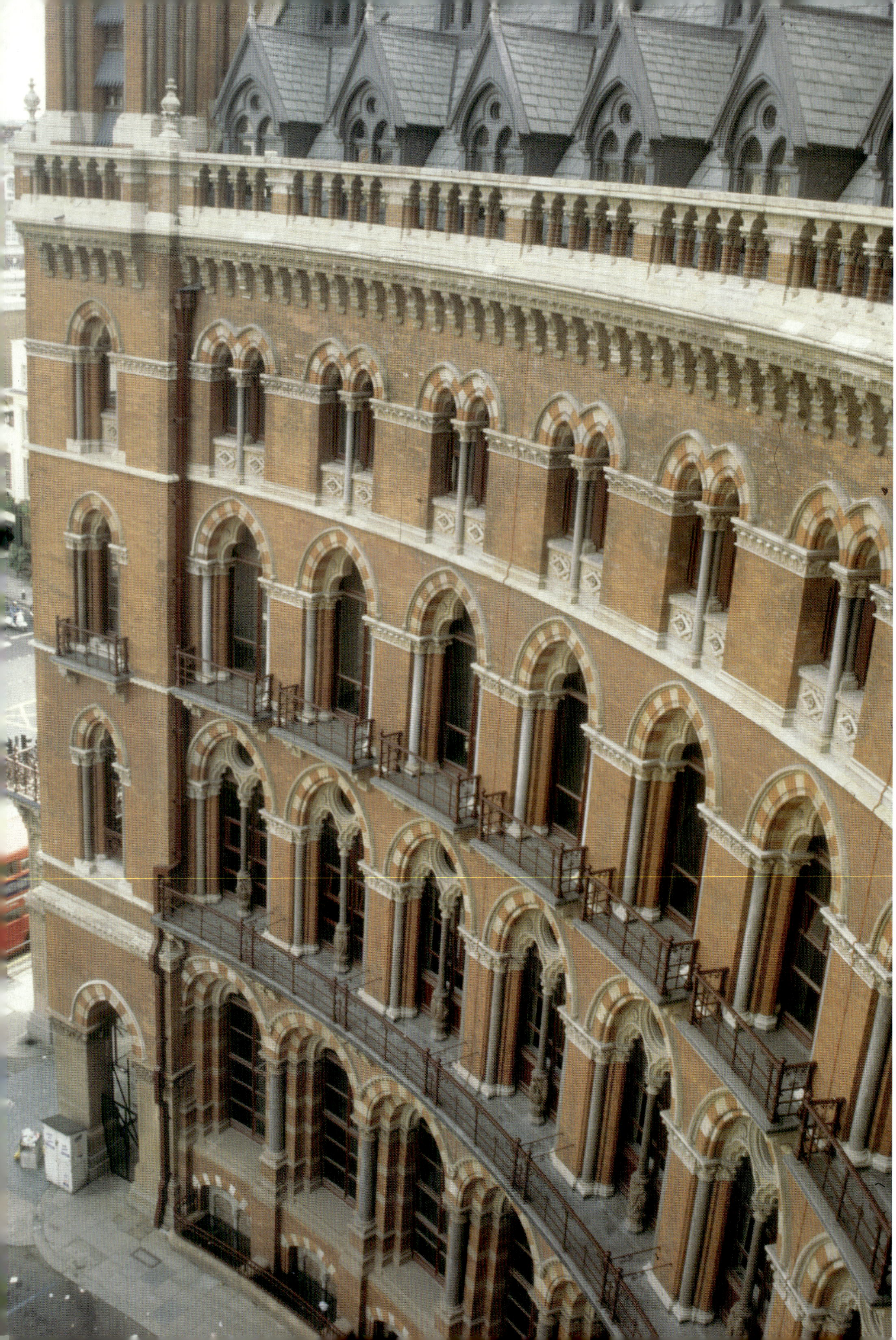

Towards Independence 1995–1999

Left: At the same time work started in earnest on the long-awaited restoration of St Pancras station, beginning with the exterior fronting Euston Road, the erstwhile Midland Hotel. It was a huge task but the attention to detail was praiseworthy. *Robin Leleux*

Right: An unusual entry, indeed a survivor from the earliest days of railway operation, was the 'policeman's cottage' above the north portal of Clayton Tunnel on the main Brighton Line. Originally for the signaller – then called a policeman, hence the nickname of 'bobby' for signallers even today – it is now renovated and available for holiday letting. *Robin Leleux*

Once the Settle & Carlisle line had been reprieved, much effort was put into enhancing its stations and passenger amenities, as a long-term programme which is still continuing. One aspect of this was better platform lighting but instead of using standard lamp posts replica Midland Railway lanterns were used, using an original as template, as here at Horton-in-Ribblesdale. The result is most effective. *Robin Leleux*

55

Memorials and Miscellaneous

Over the years a number of smaller – often fascinating – projects have been entered. With the increased consciousness resulting from the anniversaries associated with World War 1, there has also been an effort to see war memorials relating to the railway industry identified and restored.

Above: Located in churchyards across the country are a number of memorials dedicated to those who have lost their lives either in the construction or operation of railways. The churchyard of St John's in Bromsgrove incorporates this memorial to two men killed when the boiler of their engine exploded in 1840. The restoration work was Highly Commended in 2014. *Phil Howl*

Right: When the Ffestiniog Railway introduced steam operation in 1864 it also introduced a new system of marking the track with slate milestones; over the years many of these had disappeared or been damaged. From 2004 onwards the line's volunteers had sought to restore the original 1864 scheme, producing, where necessary, milestones using local slate. Their work was rewarded with the Volunteers Award in 2013. *Deborah Trebinski*

56

Memorials and Miscellaneous

Restoration Rewarded

Above: One of the most distinctive facets of the East Coast main line north of Newcastle is the provision of signs along the trackside. These had been allowed to deteriorate but a group of Network Rail staff and other volunteers undertook their restoration; their efforts were justly awarded with the Stagecoach Volunteers Award in 2018.
John Frater

Right: Situated outside Great Malvern station are two ornate cast-iron columns and lanterns; after some years of deterioration, the local town council undertook their restoration. One was found to be in good condition but the other was too badly damaged to be saved. The former was used to produce patterns to enable a replica to be produced; the end result was Highly Commended in 2011.
Paul Taylor

Memorials and Miscellaneous

HIGH WYCOMBE
FORMERLY THE JUNCTION FOR THE
MARLOW AND MAIDENHEAD LINES

MEMORIALS AND MISCELLANEOUS

Left: It's surprising what can emerge during other work; during refurbishment work at High Wycombe historic running-in boards were discovered behind more modern work. It was decided to restore *in situ* one of the BR era enamel signs and, as seen here, an even-older Great Western example. The word 'Formerly' was added to avoid confusion as, unfortunately, it has not been able to change at High Wycombe for Maidenhead since 1970. *Anthony Lambert*

Above: Whilst it was known that the Great Central Railway possessed three departmental war memorials at its Marylebone terminus, two had disappeared and one was on display at the National Railway Museum. As a result, when Chiltern Railways decided to commemorate World War 1, it undertook the creation of three replica plates; the resulting work was Highly Commended in 2015. *Richard Horne*

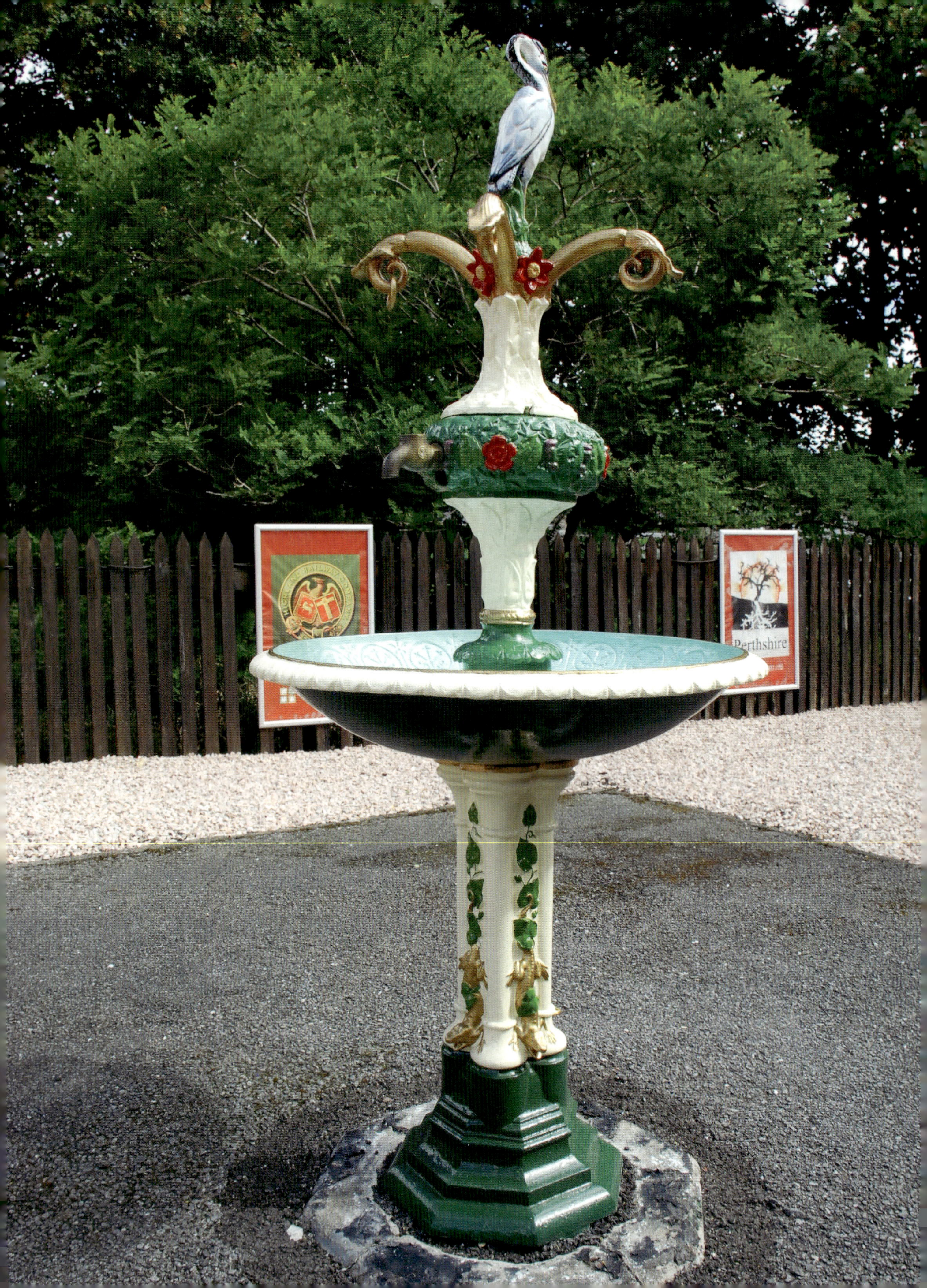
Perthshire

MEMORIALS AND MISCELLANEOUS

Left: The Highland Railway station at Pitlochry has seen a considerable amount of restoration work over the years; one of the most unusual facets of this was the work undertaken on the ornate drinking fountain, in the form of a heron, produced by Walter MacFarlane & Co of the Saracen Foundry in Glasgow. This attractive feature was Highly Commended in 2013. *John Ives*

Above: All aspects of the railway's built environment is eligible for entry; one of the more unusual – Highly Commended in 2016 – was the restoration of the line-side fencing and mileage marker entered by the Southwold Railway. *Michael Papps*

CHAPTER 5

Charitable Status 2000–2004

By the year 2000 Management Committee members were keen to achieve the full independence which charitable status would bring. As Treasurer, Mike Stanbury brought with him experience of guiding some five broadly similar organisations to the NRHA into becoming charities but the Chairman, at that time still David Morgan, stalled. Mike was not to be deflected, stressing the public benefit required for achieving charitable status, and was firmly backed by Jim Cornell at RHT who could also see the advantages in attracting additional sponsorship. The Chairman and Secretary, both senior solicitors and responsible for leading HRA, put sufficient objections forward to make the simple scheme favoured by Mike unworkable. But in practice this need not be so, as Mike was finding in his discussions with the Charity Commission.

Then came the change of Chairman, John Ellis taking over, and with his full backing, together with that of Jim Cornell, Mike was told to get on with it, resulting in constructive and productive discussions

Jim Cornell

Having joined British Railways North Eastern Region as a civil engineering student apprentice Jim Cornell rose through senior positions in the Railway Industry in a career which spanned over fifty years. From General Manager ScotRail he moved to become BRB's Director of Civil Engineering and then MD of Regional Railways. By then privatisation of the industry was imminent and he became Group Managing Director of British Rail Infrastructure Services in 1993. As well as taking on the role of Executive Director of the Railway Heritage Trust from 1996 until retirement Jim was a Non Executive Director of Railtrack PLC and then Network Rail. From his early days at the RHT Jim valued the work of the National Railway Heritage Awards, becoming a member of its Management Committee, thus enabling the two organisations to work closely together. He still maintains his keen interest in railway heritage, now as Chairman of the RHT's Board.

Right: Jim Cornell. *Duncan Phillips/NRHA*
Above: Award plaque. *Robin Leleux*

Above: The Ouse Viaduct at Balcombe (Raistrick and Mocatta 1841), carrying the Brighton Line straight as a die across the valley, is an engineering and architectural masterpiece. Its thorough restoration in the late 1990s won a special Millennium Award.
Robin Leleux

with officials at the Charity Commission. Naturally much centred on the objects of the charitable trust, the key words being preservation and education; it was accepted that this was the main focus of the trust rather than the improvement of architecture. The Commission explained that preservation is charitable when it is for the public benefit and satisfies a merit criterion.

Naturally this 'merit criterion' needed determining, based on authoritative and objective expert evidence which did not seem to be forthcoming from the awards as constituted, for any organisation could enter a building irrespective of its perceived historical or architectural value. This raised the question as to whether awards for such buildings could be charitable.

So to be charitable the Awards would need to establish guidelines for entrants to follow so that the winning buildings did meet the merit criterion, plus evidence that these had been followed. This meant that the Panel of Adjudicators needed to comprise people with the expert skills to determine this, while some of the awards themselves might need to be reconsidered.

Regarding 'public benefit' public access is one obvious requirement which might be difficult where a private building e.g. a former station converted into a house, or an operational structure like a signal box were concerned. However in such cases public access might be through printed materials, internet sites and public lectures, all properly advertised. There was also the issue of cash prizes to non-charitable bodies like public authorities and private companies. Finally the Awards' archive must be publically available if the educational criterion for charitable status was to be met.

Mike Stanbury was able to handle these fundamental queries such that the Charities Commission wrote in December 2004 that it was willing in principle to accept the Awards as charitable. It was satisfied that, following use of the detailed questionnaire by the two visiting judges at any entry, there were sufficient experts assessing the awards who could determine whether the buildings concerned were worthy of preservation. Also that the awards bring recognition of the preservation achievement and further alerts the public to both an individual building's preservation and its historic or architectural value. Public benefit was satisfied as most projects entered for the awards involve structures readily visible to the public outside; if this was not the case other forms of public access should be considered. If public access is not going to be possible in any form then it would not be appropriate for the building to receive an award. This has certainly been the case with for example a major operationally sensitive Network Rail structure, despite it occupying the well-excavated and archaeologically recorded site of early locomotive sheds.

The other special Millennium Award went to the Settle & Carlisle line's operator Northern Spirit for station regeneration, exemplified by the restoration work done at that time on Ribblehead station by the Settle & Carlisle Railway Trust. This resulted in winning the Railtrack Award. *Robin Leleux*

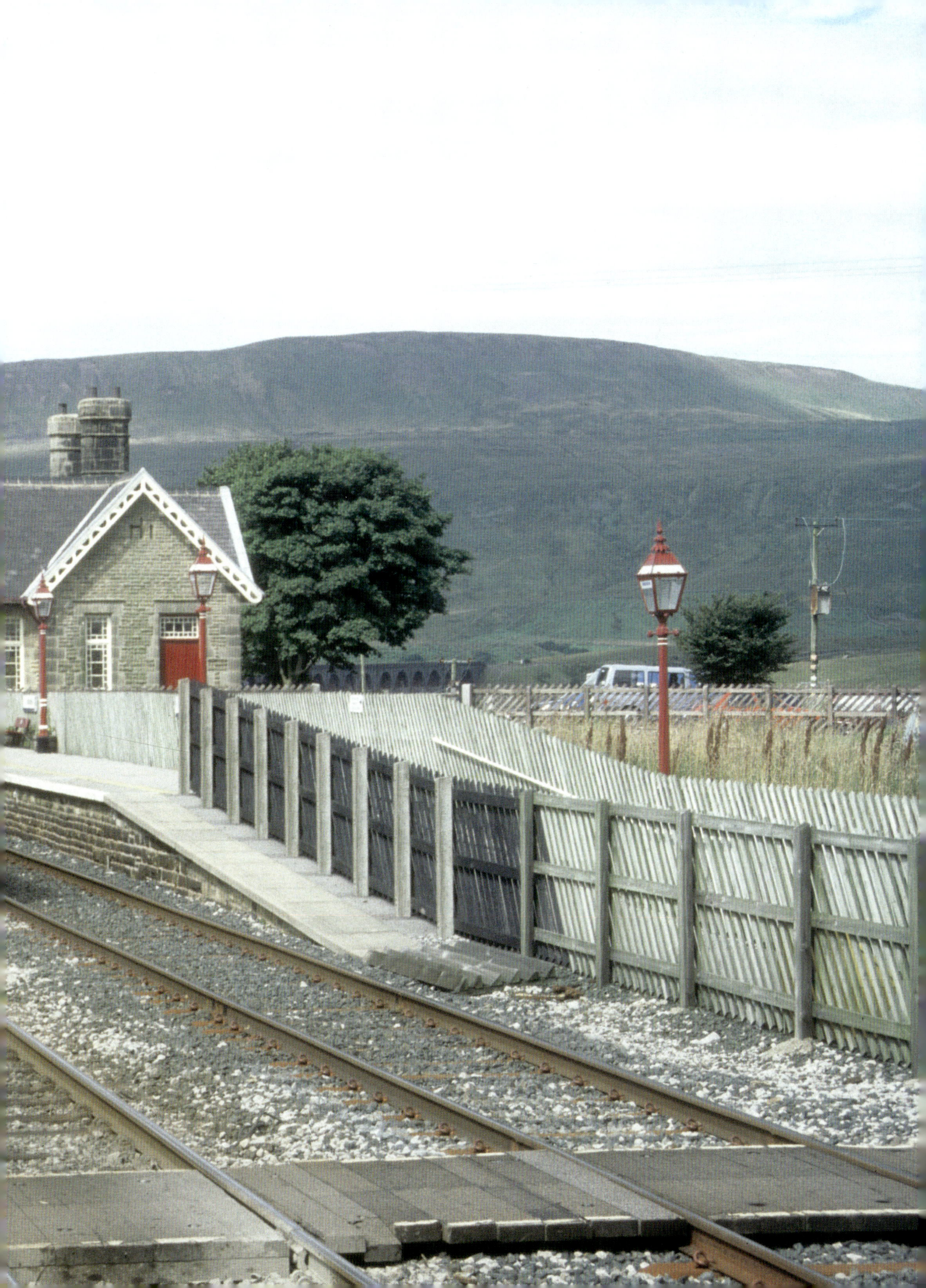

Above: The trainshed roofs at major stations are impressive reminders of Victorian engineering and grandeur, but they can be devils to maintain properly (electrification has been a great help after the steam age!). Brighton's roof by H. E. Wallis dates from 1883 and was thoroughly restored to win the *Modern Railways* Award in 2000. *Robin Leleux*

The arrangements for establishing the archive, supported by both experts from HRA and the National Museum of Science and Industry, were also approved. The upshot was that provided that the trustees agreed to an appropriately modified form of words for the objectives, more specifically related to railways, then a new trust deed should be drawn up for formal recognition. This was done and the Trust Deed was made on 16 December 2004, registration following on 25 January 2005. The Trust's objects were to apply its funds and income for:

> 1: the preservation of the buildings and infrastructure of the national railway networks of Great Britain and Ireland, past and present, whether for transport or other purposes, and for the continued benefit of the public; and

> 2: the advancement of the education of the public in railway preservation, in particular but not exclusively by the establishment and maintenance of an archive of the National Railway Heritage Awards.

The first three Founder Trustees were John Ellis, Jim Cornell and Michael Stanbury. They were initially joined by Robin Leleux, Anthony Saunders, Christopher Smyth, and Antony Tomkins. Their powers were straightforward, including composition of the Trust, holding meetings, appointing a management committee and keeping proper accounts. Significantly it allowed the Trust to raise funds and invite and receive contributions, i.e. to seek wider sponsorship which did imply moving away from dependence upon the Ian Allan publishing house. It was in this period that two significant players joined the Management Committee, both from the railway industry: Deborah Trebinski, who succeeded in running most effectively day-to-day aspects of the Awards as Awards Manager for the next twelve years, and Mike Lamport, who transformed its PR aspects.

Above: The great roof over Liverpool's Lime Street station was built in two stages between 1867 and 1879 (William Baker, Francis Stevenson and E. W. Ives, LNWR engineers) as the station continued to expand. As Biddle says: 'the combination of gentle vertical and horizontal curves provides a satisfying perspective ... enhanced by the outer gable screen'. Its restoration in 2001 won the London Underground Award. *Robin Leleux*

Below: Work on Waterloo's great roof, designed by Jacomb Hood the younger and Gilbert Szlumper, was even more complex as most key pieces of structural ironwork were of an individual length and size to fit the gentle curve of the station's platforms below. The side screens by platform 1 are not fully appreciated by the public as they are round the side but they won the First Engineering Craft Skills Award in 2004. *Robin Leleux*

So the Awards, starting life as the Best Preserved Station Competition, emerged twenty-five years later as an independent Charitable Trust, its registered number being 1107792. Sadly Michael Harris, the Awards' founding father, had died after a lengthy illness in October 2001.

Meanwhile the normal running of the Awards was proceeding smoothly, with usually over 40 entries each year (2003 was thinner at 36) of very good quality. This enabled the committee to invite leading figures to present the Awards each year, with HRH The Princess Royal prominent here in 2002. She was preceded by Sir Alastair Morton, Chairman of the Strategic Rail Authority in 2000 and Sir Neil Cossons, Chairman of English Heritage, in 2001. Then Richard Bowker, Chairman and Chief Executive of the Strategic Rail Authority came in 2003 followed by a return visit from HRH The Duke of Gloucester in 2004. By this time the ceremony was well ensconced at the Merchant Taylors' Hall in Threadneedle Street in the City of London, having arrived there in 2000.

The Awards celebrated the Millennium by having two special, one-off National Railway Heritage Millennium Awards, each awarded for significant work in heritage restoration and regeneration. The first went to the Ouse Viaduct at Balcombe on the Brighton Line (Railtrack Southern Zone), designed by J. U. Raistrick and David Mocatta, it is 'the finest in the South of England, running long, high and straight across the valley, an imposing monument to the early railway builders' concern to enhance rather than obtrude on the landscape' (Gordon Biddle). After nearly 160 years its fine stone decorative parapet with eight ornamental pavilions gracing the ends needed such thorough restoration that several of the pavilions required actual rebuilding. The other award went to the Settle & Carlisle line (Northern Spirit) for station regeneration

Below: After a lengthy period apparently unloved, the former late (1909) GWR suburban station at Birmingham Moor Street was progressively restored to full operational use by Chiltern Railways and the Birmingham Alliance to win the Railway Heritage Trust Conservation Award in 2004. *Robin Leleux*

Above: Cleaning, repainting and general restoration work at Manchester Piccadilly station, along with improvements to public facilities such as moving walkways, was a long process but in 2002 brought it the *Modern Railways* Award. It still presents a pleasingly bright and clean appearance. *Robin Leleux*

and lighting between Settle and Armathwaite, a sure sign of the great effort the train operator, the S&C Development Co and the S&C's Friends were putting into reviving the fortunes of this classic line following its reprieve eleven years previously. Earlier signs have been noted and more was to come, including Ribblehead station that same year, entered by the Settle & Carlisle Railway Trust and receiving the Railtrack Award.

Other Award winners over this period demonstrated the wide variety of entries the Awards competition was now receiving, as well as the high standards being demonstrated. Station trainshed roofs won at Brighton, Liverpool Lime Street and London Waterloo, as well as other important work at Birmingham Moor Street, Manchester Piccadilly and Newcastle Central stations. Smaller stations honoured included Bradford-on-Avon in Wiltshire, Dinas on the reviving Welsh Highland Railway, Dundalk and Carrickfergus on either side of the Irish border, Stone in Staffordshire and Hardingham in Norfolk, the latter entered privately by Michael Senatore who subsequently was able to join first the judging team then the Panel of Adjudicators. Variety was certainly evident among the signal boxes which ranged from three distinctive ones on the Newcastle to Carlisle line (Haltwhistle, Hexham and Wylam) to Birmingham New Street power box and included new works on heritage railways at Grosmont on the North Yorkshire Moors Railway, Quorn and some double tracking work on the Great Central Railway and Swanage on the Swanage Railway. Vital strengthening work sensitively done on the wooden viaduct at Moy on the Highland main line and important work on Runcorn viaduct were recognised as was the rebuilding of the distinctive Midland Railway-style drystone walling at Blea Moor on the S&C. The gentlemen's cast iron urinal at Crich Tramway Museum – a very rare survivor – was another worthy winner.

Above: The station at Bradford-on-Avon is in typical late Brunel Tudor style with warm pale cream Bath stone, steep gables and deeply overhanging canopies. It was well restored at the turn of the century to win the Railway Heritage Trust Award in 2000. *Robin Leleux*

Conversion of buildings to new uses also featured strongly, including remodelling the former goods warehouse at Goathland (North Yorkshire Moors Railway) as a distinctive tearoom (tables are placed within low-sided goods wagons) – the station's characteristic coal drops were also very well restored – installing the British Empire and Commonwealth Museum into Brunel's former trainshed at Bristol Temple Meads station, and incorporating the 1855 station building at Halifax into Eureka, the children's science museum. But overshadowing all of these was the complete transformation of Nottingham London Road Low Level station into a health and fitness centre. This imposing terminal station, built by an ambitious local company with a name longer than its finances justified but strategically placed in railway politics, had been without regular passenger services since 1944 but had survived until the 1970s as a major parcels depot. Its transformation was most imaginative, upstairs offices complete with ornate ceiling roses became treatment rooms while the main concourse housed all the machinery found in a modern gym. The free-standing wooden booking office became the weights centre while as the *pièce de résistance*, a large swimming pool sat between where the platforms once were, the cast iron beams still doing their job overhead. It justifiably received the *Modern Railways* Award in 2001.

The year 2004 of course saw the twenty-fifth anniversary of the Awards competition and to mark this leading winners from those years were honoured. There were five categories, engineering structures, buildings

CHARITABLE STATUS 2000–2004

on the National network, buildings on heritage railways, principal stations and new uses, mostly with a short list of three. Lambley Viaduct in Northumberland and the Ouse Viaduct in Sussex contested the honours with Moy Viaduct in the Highlands, the ultimate winner of the Engineering Structures Award. Among the buildings on the national network were the three signal boxes on the Newcastle to Carlisle line, the revived Mansfield station and stations on the S&C which actually won the Buildings on the National Network Award. On the heritage side the contestants were, as one might expect, Arley on the Severn Valley, Horsted Keynes on the Bluebell and Ingrow on the Keighley & Worth Valley, Horsted Keynes running out winner of the Buildings on the Heritage Railways Award. The three principal stations nominated were Brighton, Glasgow Central and Manchester Piccadilly, Glasgow Central taking the honours for the Principal Stations Award. Finally for new uses, there were four nominees, Halifax 1855 building, Goathland goods warehouse, Manchester Liverpool Road station (the original station on the Liverpool & Manchester Railway, by then part of the Manchester Museum of Science and Industry), and Nottingham London Road Low Level Station, part of Holmes Place Health Clubs, which actually won the New Uses Award.

Below: Up in Gwynedd the North Wales Narrow Gauge Railways built an interchange station with the LNWR at Dinas. When the successor railway folded in 1937 the station building managed to survive as a council store, to be successfully revived, along with the Welsh Highland Railway, in the 1990s, winning the *Railway World* Award in 2000. *Robin Leleux*

73

Restoration Rewarded

Above: Carrickfergus lies on the Belfast – Larne line in Northern Ireland, the station serving a busy town. When it was fully refurbished, new lifts for the subway were installed; not only were they much appreciated by the passengers but they were designed to fit in stylistically with the station's appearance, being Commended in 2002. *Robin Leleux*

Below: With its three prominent Jacobean-style gables, narrow multi-light mullion windows and triple-arched recessed entrance Stone station (1849) is one of the most impressive secular buildings in this old town, as well as being one of the finest of Hunt's design for the North Staffordshire Railway after Stoke-on-Trent. A jointly funded project and entered by the Town Council, its restoration in 2004 won the *Modern Railways* Award. *David Gaskin*

Above and below: The Newcastle to Carlisle line was early on the railway map but some of its distinctive signal boxes were built sixty–odd years later. Along with Hexham, the unusual box at Haltwhistle – it is jettied out on both sides of a lofty brick base – and the overhead box at Wylam were renovated and entered as a trio, winning the *Modern Railways* Award in 2003. *Robin Leleux (both)*

Restoration Rewarded

Above: The Awards do not ignore relatively modern buildings. One such needing considerable attention to its concrete structure was the iconic New Street Power Box in Birmingham, Commended in 2001. *Richard Foster*

Below: The Midland Railway had its own distinctive style of drystone walling, employing the 'buck and doe' form of cap stones, ie alternately high and low. This is evident at the north end of Ribblehead Viaduct where many of the railway's walls on Blea Moor were being repaired or even rebuilt, resulting in the First Engineering Award in 2002. *Robin Leleux*

Above: Tramways have always been included in the Awards so the rare survivor of a gentlemen's public urinal, in all its cast iron glory, was an unusual entry. Its original purpose was for the relief of tram crews; now it resides at Crich Tramway Village where it won the Virgin Trains Volunteers Award in 2004. *Robin Leleux*

Restoration Rewarded

CHARITABLE STATUS 2000–2004

Left, above and below: Goathland was originally a quiet wayside station serving an upland community on the North Yorkshire Moors. However its popularity as an important stop on the revived North Yorkshire Moors Railway, especially once filming for the popular television *Heartbeat* series had begun, meant its facilities could no longer cope. While the old coal drops were restored, the former goods shed was successfully converted into a tea room, patrons like the author's wife sitting in old trucks on the sidings. The Ian Allan Publishing Award followed in 2000. *Robin Leleux (both)*

Above: Operational requirements following reduced train services through Halifax rendered the fine 1855 station building, designed by John Butterworth, redundant. However opposite was the expanding new children's science museum 'Eureka' which has taken over the building as a museum extension, a worthy new use bringing with it the Railway Heritage Trust Award in 2001. *David Gaskin*

79

Above and below: The impressive station at Nottingham London Road Low Level had a complicated history and saw its last passenger train leave in 1944. After long use as a parcels depot it faced an uncertain future until a splendid transformation into a health and fitness centre took place. Gymnastic equipment fills the concourse, there are weights in the freestanding wooden booking office while a swimming pool occupies the space between the platforms, where the original ironwork of the roof still is evident. The *Modern Railways* Award in 2001 was justly deserved.
Robin Leleux (2)

CHARITABLE STATUS 2000–2004

Right: Thanks to the Beeching rationalisation of Nottinghamshire's railways Mansfield was left bereft, as the largest town in the UK without a passenger railway. Enlightened thinking at the end of the century saw passenger services restored through to Worksop and Mansfield station duly restored and re-opened. Fortunately its fine booking hall had survived. It won the Railway Heritage Trust Award in 2002. *Robin Leleux*

Above: Liverpool Road Station in Manchester is among the oldest in the country, although it remained open for only fourteen years, giving way to Victoria. It has survived, becoming part of the Manchester Museum of Science and Industry and as such demonstration trains are run using replicas of early locomotives such as *Planet*, a 2-2-0 of the Liverpool & Manchester Railway (1992). Originally Commended in 1983, the station was so again in the 25th Anniversary Awards. *Robin Leleux*

81

New Build

There is a considerable debate both among the judges and the adjudicators about whether the competition should examine and reward buildings that are effectively modern constructions. There are, perhaps, four facets of this. The first – effectively the dismantling and reconstruction at a new location of historic buildings – has seen a number of highly successful entries over the years. The second is a modern construction that incorporates features – such as wrought- and cast-iron work – salvaged from older buildings. The third is wholly new build but designed to replicate an historic structure that once stood on the site. And, perhaps the most contentious of all, new build that extends existing structures or is designed to complement the facilities already provided.

Above: The original Great North of Scotland station at Keith Town was demolished by British Rail in the 1970s; the preserved Keith & Dufftown Railway Association based its replica upon the original design, retaining its unusual entrance arrangement – from the higher level – as well as the primarily wooden construction.
Andy Savage

NEW BUILD

Right: With the reconstruction of the line between Toddington and Cheltenham Racecourse, the Gloucestershire – Warwickshire Railway decided to construct a replacemernt of the small Hayles Abbey Halt. Whilst using some modern construction methods, the finish – including the typical GWR 'Pagoda' – is such that it's hard to differentiate the new from the original station.
Robert Medland

Below: The same is true of the reconstructed line-side halt at Heniarth on the Welshpool & Llanfair Light Railway; this was Highly Commended in the 2018 competition.
Edward Dorricott

83

Left: An example of a new build incorporating historic features is the new waiting room constructed on the up platform at Ropley on the Mid-Hants Railway. Although the majority of the construction is new, albeit to a London & South Western design, some of the features – such as the cast-iron brackets and columns (which were salvaged from Ringwood) – are genuine. *Keith Leicester*

Below: The restoration of the various buildings on the Settle to Carlisle is a text-book case of creating a style and maintaining it throughout; indeed the style guidelines represented one of the more unusual entries that the competition has received over the years. At Settle, in order to improve waiting facilities on the up platform when the main station was closed, a new waiting shelter, built to match the existing building, was completed; it was Highly Commended in 2017. *Robin Leleux*

NEW BUILD

right: Another successful recreation of a Great Western Railway line-side station is Truthall Halt, which was entered by the Helston Railway. *Alan Hobson*

Below: An example of a wholly new build to extend the existing facilities is demonstrated by this block at Sheringham on the North Norfolk Railway. Requiring new toilet facilities, the railway had the opportunity to take over the council's existing toilets and information centre. The new structure, completed in 2016, was designed to replicate the style of the existing building whilst providing modern facilities for its users. *Theo Steel*

85

CHAPTER 6

Playing an Important Role 2004–2019

The last fundamental change to the Awards competition took place in 2004 when the distinction between the public/commercial and heritage/voluntary sectors for eligibility for certain awards was withdrawn. Also, in order to make the purpose of each named award clearer, a brief description was added, so that the overall schedule of awards now became the *Modern Railways* Restoration Award, the London Underground Accessibility Improvement Award, the Railway Heritage Trust Conservation Award, the First Engineering Craft Skills Award, the Network Rail Partnership Award, the Westinghouse Signalling Award, the Virgin Trains Volunteers Award (this alone was restricted to volunteer input, and also alone still carried a cash award, of £1,000), and finally the Ian Allan Publishing Award for the best entry of that year. Since then the sponsorship of individual awards has inevitably changed as sponsors come and go, and three more awards have been added, for urban heritage, commercial restoration and a supporters' award for small projects. The standard dark blue elliptical plaques, which had first appeared in the 1990s, were by this time standard, coming from Leander Architectural of Buxton. The list of Guests of Honour is appended.

There were inevitably changes in the Management Committee, as first Mike Lamport had to relinquish his

Above: Award plaque. *Peter Waller*

Above: Signalling needs on the North Yorkshire Moors Railway at Grosmont have grown more complex over the years, not least with regular running through to Whitby, so the opportunity to install the redundant impressive gantry from Falsgrave, Scarborough, suitably modified, was not to be missed. It duly received the Siemens Signalling Award for 2015, its plaque unveiling being the last such event Deborah Trebinski was able to attend. *Richard Tinker*

Above: The NER opened a lengthy cross country line from Northallerton across to Hawes where it met a short Midland Railway branch from Garsdale. The Wensleydale Railway aims to reopen as much of this as possible, at present using the central part west of Leeming Bar. Scruton station, on a minor road to the east, was an overlooked gem, largely untouched from LNER days when BR closed it in 1954, and the Wensleydale Railway have done a superb job in recreating that atmosphere, so receiving the Railway Heritage Trust Conservation Award in 2015. *John Young*

Above: The 'King's Cross Railway Lands' north of the main station included a large grain warehouse, potato warehouses and coal drops. The Midland Railway also had its first base here before being able to run independently into London. Long abandoned and derelict the area is being imaginatively revitalised with a range of new uses – a major college, retail outlets, housing, a leading supermarket chain – and so won the NRHA Best Entry for 2016, the award being made in memory of Deborah Trebinski who had died a few months earlier. *Robert Thornton*

PRO role thanks to pressure of work within the railway industry, heavily concentrated around King's Cross; he was replaced as PRO by Peter Waller who had worked with Ian Allan Publishing. Then early in 2010 Jim Cornell retired as Executive Director of the Railway Heritage Trust, and also from the Awards Management Committee, being replaced in both roles by Andy Savage, coming from senior positions within the rail industry as a civil engineer. John Curley was to succeed Jim as the Awards' Sponsorship Manager. At the end of 2012 David Lawrence retired as Chairman of the Adjudicators, being replaced by Robin Leleux who by then had completed twenty-one years as Chairman of the Judges. His position was filled jointly by Clive Baker and Gavin Johns. Finally, and sadly, the Awards lost its effervescent and eminently practical Awards Manager in 2016 when a virulent cancer took Deborah Trebinski. She just managed to attend the plaque unveiling at Grosmont for the newly installed signal gantry but could not manage the similar ceremony at Scruton on the Wensleydale Railway shortly afterwards. The NRHA Best Entry for 2016, won by Kier Construction and the King's Cross Partnership for their fine work on the King's Cross Midland goods shed, was dedicated to her memory. She was replaced as Awards Manager by Rob Hayward.

Judging is often a most pleasant experience but it also has its pitfalls. Ian Wright was locked (accidently one hopes!) in the Gents while judging Hertford East station while Peter Butler was invited to climb inside the clock tower at Lincoln Central. Not only was this heavily pigeon-infested but the ladder became rickety and then petered out; needless to say judging was politely terminated and it was some years before Lincoln Central re-appeared in the Awards competition. Bridges are often in rural or isolated locations, none more so than the Slatty Viaduct on the Cork to Cobh line in Ireland. Judge Douglas Ferguson, having come down from the Bangor area on the crack 'Enterprise Express' train, was offered a boat organised by IE for his inspection trip, a profitable day for both parties as the viaduct went on to win that year's First Group Skills Award (2006). Not so lucky was Robin Leleux, who had to brave lively and inquisitive bullocks while negotiating a steep and slippery muddy bank down to the River Arrow to inspect the unusual long culvert there. Roofs have their own attraction; Marion Armstrong and Robin Leleux had the opportunity to explore the new roof at Carlisle (formerly 'Citadel') station, clambering

Above: The baronial style of Lincoln Central fits well with much of Lincoln's medieval townscape. The station building and its surrounds have received more attention in recent years – the tower and its clock are evident here – as has the roof which was Commended in 2017. *RHT*

Above: Viaducts are not always easy to photograph or indeed to access; Douglas Ferguson was brought here by boat to judge Slatty Viaduct in 2006 when it won the First Group Skills Award. *Iarnród Éireann*

up by short protected ladders under the watchful gaze of Network Rail staff. Not so at Darlington North Road Museum where Robin had to inspect the new slates and flashings from a tall and insubstantial ladder. Less perilous for two judges was their escorted walk through Brunel's Thames Tunnel although the smell from ancient sewage seeping in was memorable! Finally Deborah Trebinski could enjoy the comfort of her own works train when she inspected the Ffestiniog Railway's slate milestones along the entire length of the line (see page 91).

Entry numbers remained buoyant over these fifteen years, totalling well over 700. Not all the winners (including those Highly Commended) can be mentioned; among them were (with their Award year in parentheses):

I. Stations Large and Small

Undoubtedly the most prestigious of all the large stations entered into the Awards competition over the forty years has been St Pancras. Its first triumphal appearance was in 1995 with the fine restoration of both the hotel facade and the Grand Staircase murals. Then in the new millennium the complete transformation of this iconic station was undertaken, in order to make the main platforms fit for the Eurostar trains on High Speed 1. As well as restoring Barlow's magnificent trainshed, and painting it in a fetching shade of light blue, the undercroft was opened up.

Above: Although cut back by BR from its huge nineteenth century extent, the overall roof at Carlisle, a station designed by Sir William Tite in 1847, still covers a substantial area so its replacement was a massive undertaking. While much of the ironwork could be kept, suitably cleaned and repaired, the tired glass was successfully replaced by the new ETF light and translucent material, the whole project winning the Bombardier Crossrail Urban Heritage Award in 2018. *Robin Leleux*

Originally carefully planned to house huge barrels of Burton beer, it had long become somewhat disreputable; now it houses fashionable shops and cafes. The whole graced the cover of the 2009 Awards call for entries brochure. Finally the hotel was completely refurbished in 2012. Over the road, work then started to make King's Cross a suitable partner, sweeping away the cluttered forecourt on the Euston Road, thoroughly cleaning the magnificent double arched train shed roof and adding a state-of-the art covered concourse on the western side, all completed in 2013. Finally a nice touch was to restore the 1877 public drinking fountain in the outside wall of St Pancras (2018), close to Euston Road and very popular in that hot summer.

Noteworthy work has been recognised at many other major stations including incorporating a major bus interchange into Hull Paragon station (2008) and clearing clutter from the grand sweep of Newcastle Central (2015). Overall roofs have been attended to – even replaced – at Carlisle (2018), Edinburgh Waverley (2014), Liverpool Lime Street (2011) and Paddington (2012) as a happy alternative to demolishing its span 4. Important mosaics were cleaned at Manchester Victoria (2016) while at Cambridge (2017) not only were the decorative roundels depicting college arms repaired and repainted but unsightly cabling removed, something the Awards has widely highlighted for years.

The national railway system still possesses a host of interesting stations, whether for decorative ironwork (Hellifield, 2014), artistic connections (Carnforth, 2006), architectural size (Crystal Palace 2013 which once boasted the largest internal scaffolding in the

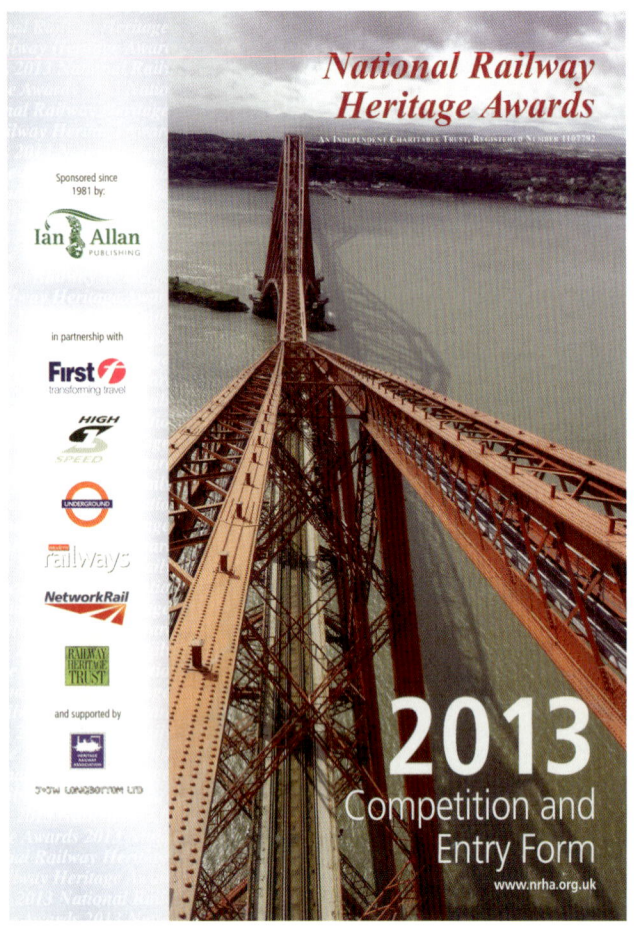

Above: The cover of the competition entry form for 2013. Until comparatively recently it was possible still to enter the competition through completion of a paper form; today, with the benefit of modern technology, all entries with support documentation are received by the judges electronically via the NRHA's website.

country), resurrection from sheer dereliction (Wakefield Kirkgate, 2015), unusual features (the decorative tiled waiting room at Worcester Shrub Hill, 2015, or the *cottage orné* design at Ridgmont in Bedfordshire 2014) or their sheer attractiveness (Wemyss Bay, west of Glasgow, 2017). The Settle & Carlisle On-line Design Guide (2013) has informed important on-going restoration and improvement work at the line's stations including Settle, Garsdale and Kirkby Stephen, while over the water Hazelhatch & Cellbridge (2009), Antrim (2015) and Helen's Bay (2013) stations stand out, the latter restored by a local beauty salon as its new premises. On the Underground the removal and careful replacement of the Paolozzi mural mosaics at Tottenham Court Road (2016) stand out, with other important refurbishment alongside operational enhancements taking place at Southgate (2008), Earls Court, Faringdon (2015) and South Kensington (2014), not forgetting similar work at James Street station in Liverpool (2016). And this is just to scratch the surface.

While the early trail-blazers on the heritage lines have largely contented themselves with keeping their stations stock in fine fettle, or adding appropriate items as finances allow, new lines have joined them with attractive stations: Consall on the Churnet Valley (2005), Kirkby Stephen East on the Stainmore Railway (2017), Stanhope on the Weardale Railway (2006) or Keith Town, long awaited on the Keith & Dufftown Railway and finally appearing in 2016. Scruton, a virtually forgotten small wayside station on the Wensleydale Railway (2015) has emerged in pristine LNER condition, more or less untouched for a generation and more while Tryfan Junction on the resurgent Welsh Highland (2014) has triumphantly emerged from a jumble of broken-down walls. The North Yorkshire Moors Railway has long been a successful entrant but perhaps its greatest triumph was the re-instatement of the fine overall roof at Pickering (2012), demolished by BR some 60 years before.

II. Bridges and Viaducts

These have always formed a distinctive set of Awards entries, although head and shoulders above the rest must be the Scottish twins, the mighty Forth Bridge (2012) and the impressively lengthy Tay Bridge (2018), and the judges were able to clamber over both, their photographs gracing the call for entries brochure and the presentation ceremony programme respectively. Moving south past Ballochmyle Viaduct in Scotland (2014), Crook O'Lune Viaduct in Lancashire (also 2014) and the twin Podgill and Merrygill viaducts (2005) on the erstwhile Stainmore route in Cumbria we cross to the impressive and historic High Level Bridge in Newcastle (2008). Among many treasures in Wales are Cynghordy Viaduct on the Central Wales line (2018) and Loughor Viaduct near Swansea (2016) where a section of the replaced timber structure has been preserved on shore as an illustration of past construction methods. Over in Ireland notable winners were the Bann Bridge near Coleraine (2013), the Three Mile Water flying junction and viaduct at Bleach Green, north of Belfast (2007), the Boyne Viaduct at Drogheda

Above: Darlington's North Road station's original train shed houses an important railway museum as well as the platform for the Bishop Auckland services. The ends of the massive oak roof trusses were failing so full re-roofing was required. In order to judge the fine slatework, and appreciate the damage caused by thieves after the replacement lead flashings, the judge had to climb a long ladder to parapet level. *Robin Leleux*

Below: Judging a series of milestones is not easy from a moving train, so for her judging trip to view its new replica slate milestones the Ffestiniog Railway kindly laid on a works train; Deborah Trebinski is seen busy at work in the company of FR staff. *Robin Leleux*

Restoration Rewarded

Above: In the 1980s when the author regularly commuted through St Pancras it was a dark and dismal place; the transformation twenty years later is both startling and fundamental, whether the opening up of the basement for good class shops, painting Barlow's magnificent roof girders sky blue, or running international trains in the main part. Small wonder that it picked up the Chairman's Special Award in 2008. *Robin Leleux*

Below: Less flamboyant than its neighbour, the station at King's Cross, designed by Lewis Cubitt, had also become very run down. Leaving aside the majestic new covered concourse, one major improvement was the thorough cleaning and re-glazing of the twin train sheds so that at last light can stream through. It too won the Chairman's Special Award, this time in 2012. *Robin Leleux*

(2016) and the Slatty Viaduct (2006) on the Cork to Cobh line.

III. Signalling

This has merited its own Award since 1990 although signal boxes did appear before then. While principally aimed at the heritage railways restoring operational signalling using traditional methods and machinery, restoration of signal box structures on the national system has also been eligible, such as Bury St Edmunds East Yard box (2006), Falsgrave box at the entrance to Scarborough station (2007, the impressive signal gantry subsequently was successfully moved to Grosmont in 2015), the mighty Severn Bridge Junction box at Shrewsbury (2010), Oakham Level Crossing box, which was the model for the Hornby Dublo version many years ago (2012), and lofty Kirton Lime Sidings box in Lincolnshire (2011). The traditional signal box is a declining species so it is worth seeking out and recording. Unfortunately some have been badly

Above: Although not a part of the original works at St Pancras, the public drinking fountain in the Pancras Road wall, dating from 1877, is a useful public amenity and its restoration to full working order in 2018, bringing it the Supporters Award for small projects, was immediately appreciated. *Robin Leleux*

Below: Praised at its completion in 1850 for the elegance of its curve, Dobson's train shed at Newcastle ultimately became cluttered, destroying the vista. Modern operating needs and changes in thinking have cleared the way once more and work at the station in 2015 brought it the London Underground Operational Enhancement Award. *Robin Leleux*

Above: Always an important station, Edinburgh Waverley has received a certain amount of attention in recent years, notably extensive work on the roof which brought it the NRHA Best Entry for 2014 Award. *John Ives*

modified: sheet zinc roofs in Scotland and appalling plate glass windows at Tram Inn in Herefordshire.

On heritage lines, the Swanage Railway, the North Yorkshire Moors and the Bluebell all stand out for innovative or progressive signalling along their lines, while the Great Central has to stand alone among heritage railways in producing first double tracking and then some quadruple tracking (at Swithland Sidings, 2012), with signalling to match. Other installations to note were Carrog (2008) on the Llangollen Railway, Holt on the North Norfolk (2009) and Woody Bay on the small Lynton & Barnstaple (2010), while Bronwydd Arms on the Gwili Railway (2011) boasts a fine pair of replica GWR level crossing gates.

IV. Other Structures

The Awards competition has always prided itself that it is open to the whole gamut of railway structures, not just stations, and varying in size from lineside mile posts (Mid Hants [2008] and Ffestiniog [2013] railways) and clocks – the Victorian clock tower by Cleethorpes station is most attractive (2018) – to whole stations, and irrespective as to whether the buildings are still in operational railway use. The early railwaymen's gravestones at Bromsgrove (2014) are well known but less so is the Britannia Bridge memorial on Anglesey (2008) and the early twentieth century locomotive fireman's gravestone at Hull (2017) with its accurate depiction of his locomotive. Static machinery can be eligible, such as the ex-BR wheel drop installed at Bridgnorth (2010). Perhaps most interesting in this category are innovative new uses for railway buildings or – at Goathland on the North Yorkshire Moors Railway – a goods van which was permanently stabled in a dock beside the station and fitted with an excellent disabled toilet, such being impossible to install in the small historic station house. Others are the Head of Steam Museum at North Road, Darlington (2008), a popular community centre incorporating cinemas,

Above: Paddington is widely acknowledged as Brunel's station masterpiece, although span four on the north side is later (1916). The threat to demolish the later span was resisted and its restoration in 2012 brought it the HS1 Station Environment Award.
Mike Ashworth

micro-brewery, shops, cafe and art gallery in the former Richmond (Yorks) station, an excellent conversion (2008), putting a comfortable home into the locomotive water tower at Settle (2013) or offices similarly at Huddersfield (2013), or transforming the vastness of Dover Marine station into a cruise line terminal (2016).

However, two projects stand high above even these. The locomotive works and shed complex at Derby dates from 1839/40 and was progressively expanded into the twentieth century. However severe rationalisation meant that it had become derelict as the twenty-first century opened. It took imagination, determination and a huge amount of money to see the potential of the complex and transform it into a vibrant college of further education. This involved a thorough restoration of the original roundhouse to show off its superb construction – it is now a college restaurant - while the carriage works has become the library. Other parts are fully in use as workshops etc and a striking new building links these two. It is superb (2011). The other is the extensive railway lands site at King's Cross, centring on the grain warehouse, other warehouses and the coal drops. The scale of this project is vast, including a college of art taking over the granary, retail and food outlets planned for the coal drops (just about completed as this book was going to press) and a Waitrose supermarket now within the former GNR potato warehouse (2016) which was also home to the Midland Railway in 1857 before it could move into its St Pancras.

So the wheel has come full circle from Sainsbury's at Bath Green Park to Waitrose at King's Cross, but assuredly it will roll on as more former railway buildings are given a new and hopefully imaginative lease of life, and entered into the Awards competition.

RESTORATION REWARDED

Left: Although lacking the fine train shed of its rival Piccadilly across town, Manchester Victoria still has architectural delights to offer, not least the mosaics installed by the L&Y Railway in 1909, along with the fine art nouveau interior and dome of the refreshment room. Their restoration, and other works at the station, were Commended in 2016. *Marion Armstrong*

Above: The early relationship between the railway and colleges in Cambridge may have been tetchy but in 1845 the Eastern Counties Railway ornamented the frontage of its grand station, designed by Francis Thompson and Sancton Wood, with roundels depicting the arms of the university and its colleges. Their painstaking restoration in 2017 earned the MTR Crossrail Urban Heritage Award. *Edward Dorricott*

PLAYING AN IMPORTANT ROLE 2004–2019

Right: The Midland Railway was a devotee of cast iron and glass at its stations as is still evident throughout the system. Hellifield station, designed by Charles Trubshaw, shows this off in spades, the decorative ironwork showing the MR's initials and wyvern insignia having again (2014) commendably been repainted. *Robin Leleux*

Above: Once the famed Crystal Palace was removed from Hyde Park to Sydenham a suitable station had to be provided for the anticipated crowds, hence the wide staircases inside the lofty building. Since being designed by Jacomb Hood in 1854 and extended by Dale Bannister and Gough in 1876, the building has had mixed fortunes but ultimately restoration in 2013 removed the huge internal scaffolding and brought with it the London Underground Operational Enhancement Award. *Richard Horne*

97

RESTORATION REWARDED

Above: If ever a station has come back from the dead it is Wakefield Kirkgate. Fifteen years ago this author had given it up for lost yet Groundwork Wakefield imaginatively persevered with a thorough restoration and even some extension of the main building, winning the Crossrail Award for Urban Heritage in 2015 in the process. (A pity about the bus shelter slap in front of the facade!) *John Ives*

Below: One of the odder features on a main line station, and an interesting survivor, is the tiled waiting room on platform 2 at Worcester Shrub Hill. Formed in cast iron from a local foundry, and clad in multi-coloured glazed tiles to form intricate patterns, the structure was carefully refurbished in 2015 and won the Great Western Railway Craft Skills Award. *Edward Dorricott*

Right: The Bedford to Bletchley line was an early branch, backed by the Duke of Bedford, which was helpful as the line passed extensively through his estates. So a distinctive *'cottage orné'* style was adopted for several of the intermediate stations which, like Ridgmont, still survive on this important but often neglected cross country route. The station's transformation into a local heritage centre in 2014 was Commended. *NRHA*

Below: Lying on the banks of the Clyde some thirty miles west of Glasgow, the Caledonian Railway's Wemyss Bay station was, and is, the embarkation point for steamers, so an appropriately extensive station was necessary. Designed originally by the railway's architect James Miller and engineer Donald Matheson in 1903, it has been expertly restored, after a period of unfortunate neglect, in a joint effort between railway and maritime interests, to win the NRHA Best Entry for 2017. *John Ives*

Restoration Rewarded

Above: The Settle & Carlisle line's stations were all of a piece, designed by J. H. Sanders (the Midland Railway's stations architect), only varying in size depending on the importance of the community served. Kirkby Stephen West exemplifies this, as seen through the equally distinctive Midland Railway footbridge. It won the Railway Heritage Trust Conservation Award in 2005. *Robin Leleux*

Below: Hazelhatch & Celbridge station dates back to 1846 but in recent years it has flourished as both a terminal point for some Dublin area suburban trains and a stopping point for trains from the Waterford and Galway lines into Dublin. It was successfully adapted in 2009 to cater for passengers with mobility problems, as such winning the London Underground Accessibility Award. *Iarnród Éireann*

Above: The present station at Antrim dates from 1901-2, rebuilt in English Domestic Revival style by Berkeley Deane Wise. The local bus depot was also a long established feature in the goods yard. Finally the two were integrated, the latter having a modern eco-friendly design alongside the refurbished Edwardian booking hall and repaired canopy, the work being Commended in 2015. *NRHA*

Below: Helen's Bay began life as a private station for the local great landowner. Situated on the outskirts of Bangor on the busy commuter line into Belfast, it was no longer used for passenger purposes but the new owner, a beauty salon, restored it to original condition and in 2013 collected the Railway Heritage Trust Conservation Award. *John Lockett*

Restoration Rewarded

Above: The celebrated mosaics by Eduardo Paolozzi, installed at Tottenham Court Road station in the 1980s, nearly became a casualty of the new Crossrail works. Instead they were carefully taken down, conserved and replaced in new positions in 2016, the meticulous work bring with it the Great Western Railway Craft Skills Award. *NRHA/LUL*

Below: The Piccadilly Line was extended north from Finsbury Park in 1932-33 and its eight new stations were designed by Charles Holden. He used either a drum-on-plinth concept, as at Southgate (Transport for London Award 2008) or the Sudbury-style 'box' as here at Turnpike Lane (Commended in 1997). *Robin Leleux*

Right above: For a short while after opening in 1863 Farringdon was a terminus for the new Metropolitan Railway but a further pair of platforms was soon added to the permanent structure which ultimately became the 'Widened Lines' from King's Cross, now the Thameslink service. The original roof was stripped back to metal, repaired as necessary and reglazed, in an exercise of 'constructive conservation'. It easily won the NRHA Best Entry for 2015. *David Jackson*

Right below: Although London's Metropolitan Railway was the first sub-surface system, Liverpool was first in the field with a deep level underground railway, linking Liverpool city centre with the Wirral on the opposite side of the Mersey; James Street was one of the first two deep level stations. Necessary repairs were effected to the stylish mosaics and other works and the MTR Crossrail Award for Urban Heritage was brought home in 2016. *John Ives*

PLAYING AN IMPORTANT ROLE 2004–2019

103

RESTORATION REWARDED

Above and left: Closer to town than its Midland counterpart, Kirkby Stephen East served the NER's Stainmore line from Co Durham into industrial Cumberland. Two train sheds covered a substantial island platform. The Stainmore Railway Co has made sterling efforts to begin the restoration of the eastern one, being Commended in 2013.

It went further in 2017 in building a new water tower and associated water crane, using recycled materials widely sourced throughout, in order to service its locomotives. This imaginative and well executed scheme won it the Contractors Restoration Award. *Robin Leleux; Marion Armstrong*

Right above: Charles Holden designed the stations for LT's Piccadilly Line extension north from Finsbury Park in 1932/33. His iconic 'drum on plinth' concept at Southgate was acclaimed by contemporaries as being 'among the finest examples of new commercial architecture built in London in the 1930s' and won the Transport for London Award in 2008. *Theo Steel*

Right below: For many years Tryfan Junction station was just decayed outer walls and piles of stones beside the revived Welsh Highland Railway, but determined volunteer effort led by the Welsh Highland Heritage Group led to its full restoration and receipt of the Volunteers Award in 2014. *Gavin Johns*

PLAYING AN IMPORTANT ROLE 2004–2019

RESTORATION REWARDED

Above: This book has recorded several overall roofs being repaired or even totally reglazed, but the total reinstatement of the overall roof at Pickering, taken down by BR over 60 years ago, was a first, especially for a heritage railway. The attention to detail was especially noteworthy even if a NER purist might object to a SR locomotive in the picture! Little surprise then that this project collected the Ian Allan Publishing Award for the best entry in 2012. *Robin Leleux*

Left: The rustic charm of Ballochmyle Viaduct in its setting was recognised by artists 150 years ago. The challenge for Network Rail was to bring the structure up to twenty-first century operating standards to allow faster freight trains, work which also brought the London Underground Operational Enhancement Award in 2014. *Geoffrey Beecroft*

Above and below: There is maintenance and there is a programme of planned major refurbishment using the most modern materials that will reduce the need for routine maintenance in the future. Both these iconic bridges benefited from the latter and our judges were privileged to be able to gain access to parts not normally available, as the photographs show. The Forth Bridge work collected the Chairman's Special Award in 2012 and the Tay Bridge the NRHA Best Entry for 2018, the latter made in tribute to the late Sir William McAlpine Bt. *Andy Savage/Edward McGloin*

Restoration Rewarded

Above: The Lune is a sinuous river as it nears its estuary and the old Midland Railway route to Lancaster crossed the great horseshoe bend at Crook O'Lune twice in a couple of hundred yards. Now a pedestrian and cycle way, the western viaduct was tired and needed some deep seated attention in 2014; the effectiveness of this brought the Restoration Award. *Oliver Doyle*

Right: The NER's Stainmore route over the Pennines involved serious civil engineering, with some viaducts being built in lattice iron – now sadly gone – and others in masonry, such as the twins Podgill and Merrygill behind Kirkby Stephen. Both are now accessible on foot and cycle ways and have been Commended. Podgill is illustrated from the end of the foot path. *Duncan Wheeler*

Above: Robert Stephenson's High Level Bridge in Newcastle (1849) was one of the engineering triumphs of an heroic age, combining a railway over a roadway and linking Newcastle (and the north) more directly with the south. The colour scheme employed in the restoration works reflect the original and the whole project won the 2008 First Group Craft Skills Award. *Dr W. Fawcett*

Below: Although not directly in the public eye, being situated on the Central Wales line and away from the nearest main road in deepest Carmarthenshire, Cynghordy is a significant structure, being the largest on the route and rising to a maximum height of 102 feet. Its restoration is also significant for the well being of the line and brought the BAM Nuttall Structures Restoration Award for 2018. *Edward Dorricott*

RESTORATION REWARDED

Above: The point was made earlier (see page 90) that wooden viaducts have progressively been replaced by steel or concrete as the timber members started to fail. Such was the case with the Loughor Viaduct near Swansea, but in an inspired move, a section of the old has been preserved nearby so that the earlier construction can be appreciated, and as such was Commended in 2016.
Richard Foster

110

Above: The Bann Bridge in Coleraine has had a chequered history as it was built in 1860 after the lines from Belfast and Derry/Londonderry. The present structure from 1924 is the only Strauss underhung bascule bridge in the UK and still regularly opens and closes for the passage of vessels. Work on it was Commended in 2013. *Douglas Ferguson*

Right: The viaduct over the River Boyne at Drogheda was another with a chequered history, not being permanently completed until 1855, thus linking Drogheda with Dublin. It was reconstructed in its present form between 1930 and 1932, thus allowing faster and heavier trains on the key Dublin – Belfast run. Further refurbishment and repair work was Commended in 2013. *NRHA*

Above and right: Refurbishment of operational signal boxes on the national system, often with improved facilities for the signaller, has been as eligible for the Signalling Award as the restoration of operational signalling systems using traditional methods on heritage railways. Prominent among the many which have appeared in the Awards competition are the huge ex-LNWR box of 1903 at Shrewsbury Severn Bridge Junction (now the largest operational signal box remaining on the national system, and Commended in 2010) and the lofty Railway Signalling Co/MS&LR box of 1886 at Kirton Lime Sidings in Lincolnshire (Commended in 2011). *Edward Dorricott, Richard Foster*

Right: The Swanage Railway has progressively installed operational signalling using traditional equipment and either restored or built new signal boxes, and is no stranger to success in the Awards competition. The new box at Corfe is a replica in LSWR/SR style, the original having been pulled down by BR in 1956, with frames from Broadstone and Brockenhurst. It won the Signalling Award in 2011; other sites on the line following in later years. *Edward Dorricott*

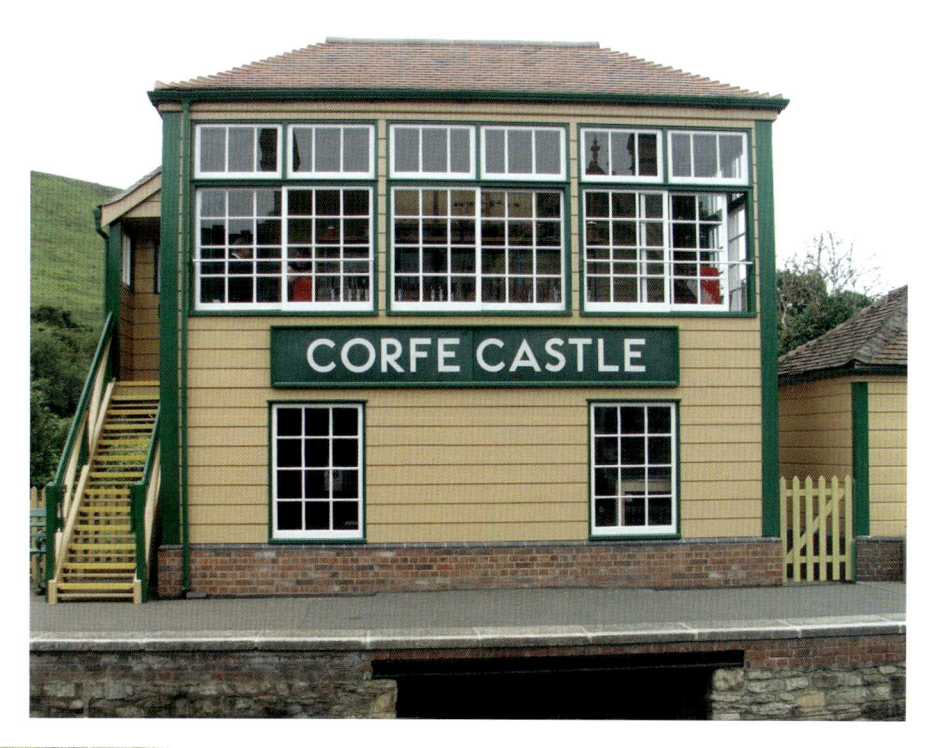

Above: The North Yorkshire Moors Railway has become increasingly busy which brings its own operating challenges, not least the 13-mile single-track section between Goathland and New Bridge, outside Pickering. New electronic technology has been used to solve the logistical issue while keeping the heritage ambience beloved of visitors. Levisham signal box, protecting the important crossing place, can be switched in or out as required, enhancing this new flexibility. So the Signalling Award for 2017 inevitably flowed that way. *Andy Savage*

113

Restoration Rewarded

Left: Unlike most heritage railways the Great Central Railway at Loughborough set out from its inception to recreate a main line, based on its pre-grouping namesake. Double track was eventually laid while at Swithland Sidings it went one better; it re-laid the passing loops either side and erected an impressive array of signals, as might originally have been found on the southern stretches of this erstwhile main line, a most important project in the heritage sector which won the NRHA Signalling Award in 2012.
Richard Foster

Playing an Important Role 2004–2019

Left: The Bluebell Railway too has had to handle increased traffic flows over recent years which has necessitated both revamping its 1882 'Brighton type 1' signal box at Horsted Keynes and its mechanicals as well as alterations down the line at Sheffield Park. The railway collected the Signalling Award two years in succession in 2017 and 2018. A vintage train passes the impressive box as it runs into Horsted Keynes with a SR bracket signal for added interest. *Fred Garner*

Below: Deep in south west Wales the small Gwili Railway needed to replace its life expired level crossing gates at Bronwydd Arms. Despite financial constraints, it was able to fabricate and install appropriate GWR-pattern single gates with both technical expertise and attention to detail, this being recognised by the NRHA Volunteers Award in 2011. *Edward Dorricott*

115

Above: Towards the end of the nineteenth century the Manchester, Sheffield & Lincolnshire Railway began to develop Cleethorpes as a seaside resort for its industrial hinterland. The station was expanded and the ornate clock tower built; this soon became a prominent landmark on the seaside promenade. After 130 years the sea air had taken its toll and the edifice needed a thorough rebuilding which was most effective, winning the Great Western Railway Craft Skills Award in 2018. *John Ives*

Above: Working on the railway has always been attended with danger and a collision in 1905 at Ulleskelf on the NER near York cost the engine crew their lives. The fireman, Edward Booth, is commemorated with a fine headstone in the cemetery near Botanic Gardens in Hull, his locomotive, 4-4-0 No 85, being accurately depicted. The re-erection and conservation of this memorial in 2017 was Commended. *Robin Leleux*

Left: Many heritage railways, being originally branch or at best secondary routes, are now carrying passengers in numbers beyond the wildest dreams of their promoters, so of course their station facilities were never built to cope and often sites are too restricted to allow expansion. In facing this problem at popular Goathland, the North Yorkshire Moors Railway hit on the novel idea of mooring a goods van permanently beside the goods shed (now a cafe, see page 78) properly fitted out as a disabled toilet, thus in 2006 winning the London Underground Accessibility Award. *NYMR*

Above: The Awards can interpret 'structures' widely to include static machinery which is how the important wheel drop on the Severn Valley Railway could be entered and win the First Group Craft Skills Award in 2010. It was redundant at Leicester locomotive depot and the SVR saw a great opportunity for the heritage sector, installing it in its workshops at Bridgnorth. *Peter Waller*

Right: G. T. Andrews built a fine terminal station at Richmond whose branch line sadly failed to survive the Beeching rationalisation. The building happily survived as a garden centre and when that finally closed was taken over by the local community as a hub. Its transformation is glorious, being intelligently and carefully done and widely popular, as the car park shows. It received the Ian Allan Publishing Award for the best entry of 2008.
Robin Leleux

RESTORATION REWARDED

Above and right: People converting unlikely buildings into homes is now the stuff of popular television programmes, but reality can be tough. The imposing water tower at Settle is one such example and the interior 'before' picture gives an idea of just what has to be done. The end result though was well worth it, with fine views from the tank floor conservatory and 'all mod cons' in a discreet extension at the rear, greatly Commended in 2012. *Robin Leleux (both)*

PLAYING AN IMPORTANT ROLE 2004–2019

Right: It is unlikely though that the station authorities at Huddersfield would welcome their fine water tower becoming a home. It became an office complex instead, appropriately for ACoRP, the body which supports rural railway development, and its conversion won the Network Rail Partnership Award for 2013. *Richard Tinker*

Right: Among the many important railway buildings transformed into new use the Derby Roundhouse complex stands out. With original buildings dating back to the beginnings of the railway era, but derelict in the early twenty-first century, a feat of great imagination has transformed it into thriving Derby College where students use original workshops, study in a library created within the original carriage shop or relax in the great locomotive roundhouse. Public visits can be arranged and are well recommended. Unsurprisingly this great project won the Ian Allan Publishing Award for best entry in 2011. *Peter Butler*

119

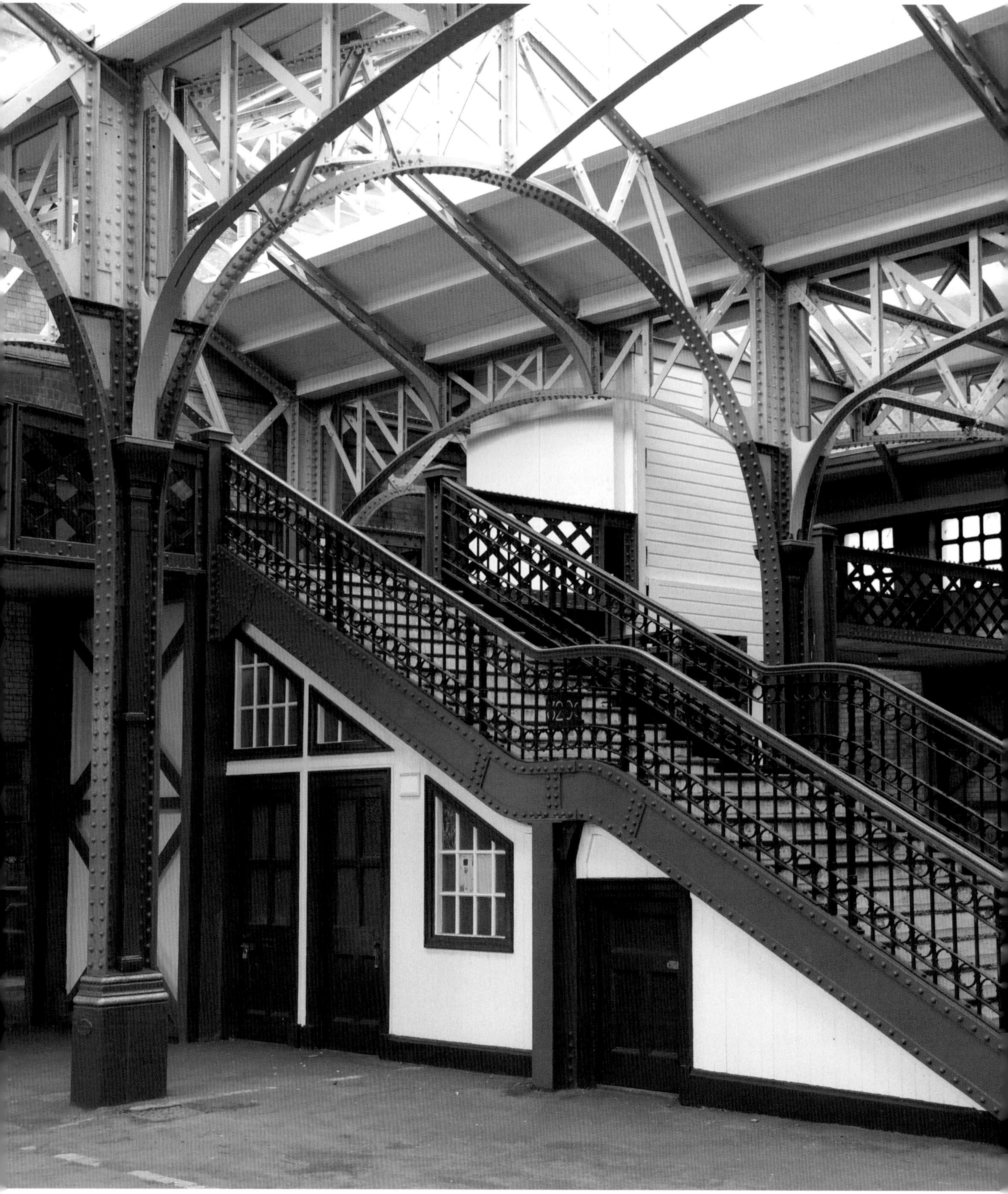

Left: Changes in travel patterns can leave former important railway buildings bereft of operational use and, as so often in the wake of the Beeching rationalisation, at the mercy of land developers. Fortunately the grand Dover Marine station, victim of the Channel Tunnel, has become a cruise line terminal instead, bringing its refurbishment and transformation the Taylor Woodrow Partnership Award in 2016. *Fred Garner*

Above: Looking over the shelves in Waitrose's supermarket to the nineteenth century girders of the former Midland Railway good shed and GNR potato warehouse at King's Cross (see page 80), retained within the glass walls of this well developed site (see page 87), the point is well made that redundant railway structures need not be lost but can be sympathetically converted to new use when the will is there. *Robin Leleux*

Plaque Unveilings

Following each year's award ceremony, the winners are encouraged to hold some form of formal unveiling of their plaque as a reminder to future generations of the entrants' success in the competition.

Above: One of the earlier plaque unveiling ceremonies was held on the Mid-Hants Railway to mark the success of Ropley station in the 1981 competition. *Courtesy Mid-Hants Railway*

Above: The plaque awarded to Pivovar Tap for the conversion work at Sheffield into the Sheffield Tap in the 2010 competition was officially unveiled on 15 February 2011. With the unveiled plaque from left to right are Andy Savage, Director of the Railway Heritage Trust and Trustee of the National Railway Heritage Awards, John Holdsworth, of Pivovar Tap Ltd, Jamie Hawksworth, of Pivovar Tap Ltd, and the then Lord Mayor of Sheffield, Councillor Alan Law JP.

Above: Keith Theobald, Chairman of the Narrow Gauge Railway Museum Trust, and Chris Smyth, HRA representative on the committee of the National Railway Heritage Awards, in front of the newly unveiled plaque at Twywn on Wednesday 16 October 2013. Chris is keeping a very firm grip on the Welsh flag; such was the strength of the wind that nature unveiled the plaque in advance of the formal ceremony! *Peter Waller*

Above: The official party after the unveiling of the plaque at Ladybank on 18 May 2016; the award was announced in December 2015 and recognised the work undertaken on the laird's waiting room a the station. From the left Andy Savage, Director of the Railway Heritage Trust, Chris Smyth, of the Heritage Railway Association and a Trustee of the National Railway Heritage Awards, Patricia O'Neill, Chair of the Ladybank Development Trust, Colin Whyte, SCRF Fund Manager for ScotRail, Christine May, Chair of the Fife Historic Buildings Trust, John Ellis, Chairman of the National Railway Heritage Awards, and John Cameron, owner of 'A4' Pacific No 60009 *Union of South Africa*. *John Yellowlees*

Above: Worksop station was awarded the Railway Heritage Trust Award in the 2018 competition. The plaque at Worksop station was officially unveiled in the station by the local MP on 12 July 2019 and is pictured here its with, left to right, Tim Brunt, Network Rail, Andy Savage, Director of the Railway Heritage Trust, John Mann MP, Theo Steel, Trustee from the National Railway Heritage Awards, and Dean Howard, from Northern.

APPENDIX 1

Presentation Ceremony Venues and Guests of Honour

Competition Year	Ceremony Year	Venue	Guest of Honour
1979	1980	Euston	Sir Peter Parker, Chairman, BRB
1980	1981	Euston	Sir Peter Parker, Chairman, British Rail
1981	1982	Euston	Sir Peter Parker, Chairman, British Rail
1982	1983	222 Marylebone Road	Sir Peter Parker, Chairman, British Rail
1983	1984	222 Marylebone Road	Robert Reid, Chairman, British Rail
1984	1985	222 Marylebone Road	Robert Reid, Chairman, British Rail
1985	1986	Unrecorded	David Shepherd, artist
1986	1987	RSA	HRH Prince Michael of Kent
1987	1988	Stationers' Hall	Sir Greville Spratt, Lord Mayor of London
1988	1989	Stationers' Hall	Lord Montagu of Beaulieu, Chairman, English Heritage
1989	1990	Unrecorded	Sir Robert Reid, Chairman BRB
1990	1991	RSA	Sir Bob Reid, Chairman BRB
1991		No competition while calendar for competition year altered	

Competition Year	Venue	Guest of Honour
1992	Unrecorded	HRH Duke of Gloucester
1993	Unrecorded	Sir Bob Reid, Chairman BRB
1994	Glaziers' Hall	Christopher Walford, Lord Mayor of London
1995	RIBA	Chris Green, Chief Executive, English Heritage
1996	RIBA	John Swift QC, Rail Regulator
1997	NRM	James Sherwood, President, Sea Containers Ltd
1998	RIBA	Glenda Jackson MP, Minister of Transport
1999	Stationers' Hall	Rt Hon Clive Martin, Lord Mayor of London
2000	MTH	Sir Alastair Morton, Chairman, Strategic Rail Authority
2001	MTH	Sir Neil Cossons, Chairman, English Heritage
2002	MTH	HRH The Princess Royal
2003	MTH	Richard Bowker, Chairman and Chief Executive, Strategic Rail Authority
2004	MTH	HRH Duke of Gloucester
2005	MTH	John Armitt, Chief Executive, Network Rail
2006	MTH	Chris Green, Chairman, Railway Forum
2007	MTH	Rt Hon Gwyneth Dunwoody MP, Chair, Transport Select Committee
2008	MTH	Paul Atterbury, antiques expert, television presenter and author
2009	MTH	Lord Adonis, Secretary of State for Transport
2010	MTH	Pete Waterman, record producer and television presenter
2011	MTH	Rt Hon David Wootton, Lord Mayor of London
2012	MTH	Simon Jenkins, Chairman, the National Trust

2013	MTH	Loyd Grossman, television presenter and gastronome
2014	MTH	Sir Peter Hendy, Commissioner, Transport for London
2015	MTH	Lord Faulkner of Worcester
2016	MTH	Paul Maynard MP, Rail Minister
2017	MTH	Mark Wild, Managing Director, London Underground
2018	MTH	Mark Carne, Chief Executive, Network Rail 2014-2018

MTH – Merchant Taylors' Hall
NRM – National Railway Museum
RIBA – Royal Institute of British Architects
RSA – The Royal Society of Arts, John Adam Street, London

Above: The Guest of Honour for the 1987 ceremony, held in the Royal Society of Arts, was HRH Prince Michael of Kent seen here presenting the brass plaque for Wellingborough station. Looking on in the background is Capt Peter Manisty of the ARPS, one of the founding fathers of the competition in the late 1970s. *Courtesy of David Allan*

Above: The winner of the *Modern Railways* Restoration Award in 2009 was Places for People for work undertaken at Wolverton. Seen with the plaque at the ceremony is Ian Troughton from Places for People with, on the left, James Abbott, editor of *Modern Railways* and, on the right, Lord Adonis, Minister of Transport, who was that year's guest of honour. *Duncan Phillips/NRHA*

Above: The Guest of Honour in 2014 was Sir Peter Hendy, the then Commissioner of Transport for London and now the Chairman of Network Rail. He is seen here on the left with John Ellis, Chairman of the NRHA on the right, with, in the centre, John Fillis and Kim Whalley of Lancashire County Council, which had won the Restoration Award in that year's competition for Crook O'Lune East Viaduct. *Duncan Phillips/NRHA*

Above: The master of ceremonies of the award ceremony for many years has been Steven Brindle of English Heritage, who is one of the country's leading authorities on the life and work of Isambard Kingdom Brunel. Amongst his publications is the definitive history of one of Brunel's most important buildings: *Paddington Station: Its History and Architecture*. *Duncan Phillips/NRHA*

APPENDIX 2

Sponsors

The first competition in 1979 was sponsored jointly by the Travel Britain Co and Ian Allan Ltd. British Rail paid for the winner's plaque. Many organisations and firms connected with the rail industry have supported the Awards over the succeeding 40 years. An asterisk * denotes sponsors for 2019.

Abellio *
Amey *
Association of Railway Preservation Societies, later Association of Independent Railways and Preservation Societies, then Heritage Railway Association *
Association of Train Operating Companies
Babcock
Balfour Beatty
BAM Nuttall *
Bombardier Crossrail
British Coal
British Rail
Carillion
Colas Rail
Costain Ltd *
Crossrail
First Engineering
First Group
GNER
Great Western Railway *
Hendy & Pendle Charitable Trust *
High Speed 1
Ian Allan Ltd (later Ian Allan Publishing Ltd)

J & J. W. Longbottom Ltd
Keighley & Worth Valley Railway
Key Publishing
London Underground (later Transport for London) *
MTR Crossrail
National Express (East Coast)
National Railway Museum
Network Rail *
National Rail Contractors' Group
Railway Heritage Committee
Railway Heritage Trust *
Railway Property Regeneration *
Railtrack
South Eastern *
Stagecoach Group *
Taylor Woodrow
The Arch Company *
Travel Britain Co
Virgin Trains
Volker Rail *
Westinghouse Brake & Signal Ltd (later Westinghouse Rail Systems, then Invenseys Rail, now Siemens)

APPENDIX 3

Judges and Adjudicators

NOTE in the first couple of years those who made the decisions regarding the winner and others to be commended were referred to as the Judges but soon they became referred to as the Panel of Adjudicators to differentiate them from those – the Judges – who actually went to each entry and reported back on it.

In the following, 1979 denotes those who formed the first group of Judges in 1979; * denotes those sitting on the Panel of Adjudicators in 2018. The others named have served as an Adjudicator at some stage during the intervening years.

David Allan (Honorary)
Michael Ashworth (London Underground) *
Clive Baker (Joint Chairman of Judges) *
Gordon Biddle (author and historian) (1979)
Marcus Binney (Chairman, SAVE our heritage campaign) (1979)
Peter Bird (architect, Travel Britain Co) (1979)
Tim Cantell (Assistant Secretary [Environment], Royal Society of Arts)
Rex Christiansen (author and historian)
Christopher Costelloe (Victorian Society) *
Dr Ian Dungavell (Victorian Society)

Michael Harris (editor, *Railway World*) (1979)
John Hume (Historic Scotland)
Louisa Humm (Historic Scotland) *
John Ives (railway architect) *
Gavin Johns (Joint Chairman of Judges)*
Bernard Kaukas (Director-Environment, BRB) (1979)
Mary King (English Heritage)
David Lawrence (Director, BR Property Board)
Frank Lawrie (Historic Scotland)
Robin Leleux (author and historian) *
David Lloyd (Victorian Society)
Candida Lycett-Green (journalist)
Capt Peter Manisty RN (Honorary) (ARPS)
Prof Marilyn Palmer (Leicester University) *
David Pearce (secretary, Society for the Protection of Ancient Buildings)
Oliver Pearcey (English Heritage)
Michael Senatore (railway architect) *
Leslie Soane (Executive Director, Railway Heritage Trust)
Daniel Sooman (Scotrail) *
Theo Steel (National Express East Anglia) *
Dr Michael Stratton (University of York)
Gavin Watson (Pevsner Books Trust) *
James Wyatt (Regional Architect, LM Region)

David A. Lawrence (1935–2017)

Joined BR Estates in 1960 and remained with property until retirement in 1992. He was enthusiastic about all aspects of railways, especially their historic development, buildings and signalling, amongst many other wide interests. David believed in the ability of buildings, well conserved and presented, being able to contribute and function in a modernising rail network. He saw the NRHA as the ideal way to promote excellence in the built railway environment.

Right: David A. Lawrence MBE FRICS

Index of Locations

222 Marylebone Road 10, 122
Aberdour 12
Alresford 14, 15
Alston 50
Antrim 101
Appleby 8
Arley 7, 9, 11, 18, 73
Aviemore 4, 46
Baker Street 21
Balcombe 65, 70, 73
Ballochmyle 90, 106
Bangor 48, 87
Barons Court 47, 49
Bath 14, 95
Beamish 9, 11
Birmingham Moor Street 70, 71
Birmingham New Street 71, 76
Blackburn 47
Blackheath 14
Blea Moor 71, 76
Bleach Green 90
Bo'ness 18

Boat of Garten 9
Bodiam 39
Bolton Abbey 47
Boston 17, 18
Bradford-on-Avon 71, 72
Braintree 47
Bridgnorth 94, 117
Brighton 68, 71, 73
Bristol 72
Britannia Bridge 94
Brockford 30, 31
Bromsgrove 56, 94
Bronwydd Arms 94, 115
Bury St Edmunds 47, 93
Cambridge 89, 96
Carlisle 87, 89
Carnforth 89
Carrickfergus 71, 74
Carrog 94
Chappel & Wakes Colne 15
Charlbury 11
Cheddleton 11

Chesham 31, 33
Clayton 48, 49, 55
Cleethorpes 94, 116
Clitheroe 46
Cobh 87, 93
Coleraine 90, 111
Combe 36
Consall 90
Corfe Castle 47, 113
Cork 87, 93
Cranmore 21, 30
Crewe 26
Crich 27, 30, 71, 77
Crook O'Lune 90, 108
Crystal Palace 89, 97
Currour 12
Cynghordy 90, 109
Damems 18, 44, 46
Darlington 17, 88, 91, 94
Derby 95, 119
Didcot 26
Dinas 71, 73

Above: Ramsgate was one of two similar designs in 1926 built for the Southern Railway north-east Kent modernisation scheme, the other being Margate. James Robb Scott had emerged as Architect for the Southern Railway having worked previously for the LSWR although Edwin Maxwell Fry was involved in the design, before he moved to a distinguished career in non-railway practice. The station entrance halls draw on contemporary US practice. Both Margate and Ramsgate were shortlisted in the 2018 competition.

Above: The Grade II listed station at Surbiton, completed in 1938, is one of James Robb Scott's later designs for the Southern Railway that paralleled those of Charles Holden for the Underground. It was restored during 1998 and 1999 and, in an era before entries were shortlisted, the work undertaken was very well-received.
Robin Leleux

Dolgoch Falls   19
Dover   95, 121
Downpatrick   32
Drogheda   90, 111
Dundalk   71
Dunrobin   46
Dunster   45, 46
Eardisley   31
Earls Court   90
Edge Hill   11
Edinburgh   89, 94
Errol   30
Exeter West   26
Falsgrave   93
Farringdon   90, 102
Fencote   19
Forth Bridge   90, 107
Foulridge   27, 30
Garsdale   90
Gisburn   37
Glasgow Central   15, 73
Glaziers' Hall   27, 123
Gloucester Road   31, 33
Goathland   72, 73, 79, 94, 116
Gobowen   18, 31
Great Malvern   18, 58
Grosmont   29, 31, 71, 86, 87, 3
Hadlow Road   9
Halifax   72, 73, 79
Haltwhistle   71, 75
Hardingham   71
Harpenden   9
Haven Street   18
Hayles Abbey   84
Hazelhatch & Cellbridge   90, 100
Helen's Bay   90, 101
Hellifield   89, 97
Heniarth   83
Hertford   87
Hexham   71
High Wycombe   61
Highley   11, 18
Holt   94
Horsted Keynes   7, 9, 11, 73, 115
Horton-in-Ribblesdale   49, 55
Huddersfield   23, 95, 119
Hull   17, 89, 94, 116
Humberstone Road   47, 48
Ilderton   46
Ingrow   27, 30, 73
Isfield   31
James Street   90, 102
Keighley   18
Keith   82, 90
Kidderminster   19, 20, 26
Kingscote   29, 31
Kingsley & Froghall   19, 20

Kingswear   31
Kirkby Stephen   90, 100, 104
Kirton   93, 112
Ladybank   13
Lambley   47, 50, 73
Laxey   29
Leamington Spa   24
Leeds   47, 51
Levisham   45, 46, 113
Lewes   16, 17, 31, 37
Lincoln   38, 46, 87, 88
Littlehempston   31
Liverpool Lime Street   69, 71, 89
Llanuwchllyn   21
London Euston   10, 11, 43, 122
London King's Cross   17, 86, 87, 89, 92, 95, 121
London Liverpool Street   17, 34, 35
London Marylebone   61
London Paddington   89, 95
London St Pancras   17, 48, 52-54, 88, 89, 92, 93, 95
London Waterloo   69, 71
Loughor   90, 110
Lyme Regis   14
Malahide   32
Manchester Central   14
Manchester Liverpool Road   73, 81
Manchester Piccadilly   71, 73, 96
Manchester Victoria   8, 11, 17, 89, 96
Mansfield   73, 81
Meldon   49
Merchant Taylors' Hall   70, 123, 124
Merrygill   90
Middleton Top   9
Millstreet   48
Montrose   14
Moy   71, 73
Muston   26
National Railway Museum   43, 123
Newark Castle   23
Newcastle upon Tyne   17, 71, 89, 90, 93, 108
North Woolwich   15
Nottingham   43, 46, 47, 72, 73, 80
Oakham   93
Oakworth   5, 6, 8, 11, 18, 26
Oswestry   31
Ouseburn   38
Pickering   90, 106
Pitlochry   63
Podgill   90, 108
Quorn   71
Radstock North   26
Ramsbottom   31, 32
Ramsgate   127
Rawtenstall   31

Reading   24
Ribblehead   28, 30, 66. 71
Richmond (Yorks)   95, 117
Ridgmont   90, 99
Robertsbridge   39
Ropley   10, 11, 84
Ross-on-Wye   19
Rowden Mill   19
Rowley   9, 11
Royal Institute of British Architects   43, 123, 124
Royal Society of Arts   10, 27, 123, 124
St Denys   15
Salford   30
Saltaire   14
Scarborough   93
Scotscalder   30, 48
Scruton   86, 87, 90
Settle   84, 90, 95, 118
Sheffield   24,30
Shenton   47
Sheringham   85
Shrewsbury   18, 19, 93, 112
Slatty   87, 88, 93
Smardale Gill   35
South Kensington   90
Southgate   90, 105
Stanhope   90
Stationers' Hall   27, 43, 122
Staverton   11
Stoke-on-Trent   31, 32
Stone   71, 74
Surbiton   127
Swanage   71
Swanwick   47
Swithland   94, 114
Tain   25
Tan-y-Bwlch   40
Tavistock   13
Tay Bridge   90, 107
Three Mile Water   90
Tottenham Court Road   90, 102
Truthall   85
Tryfan   90, 104
Turnpike Lane   102
Wakefield   90, 98
Wellingborough   14, 15, 16
Welshpool   31
Wemyss Bay   28, 30, 48, 90, 99
Westhouses   47, 52
Whitehead   46, 48
Woody Bay   94
Worcester   90, 98
Worksop   31
Wylam   71, 75
Wymondham   46
York   25